TABLE OF CONTENTS

SECTION 7: FREEZING

SECTION 8: STATE FAIR FAVORITES: BLUE RIBBON RECIPES

Excerpts Taken from:

"So Easy to Preserve" Fifth Edition, Cooperative Extension - The University of Georgia. Revised by Elizabeth L. Andress, Ph.D. and Judy A. Harrison, Ph.D. 2006

"USDA Complete Guide to Home Canning" Agriculture Information Bulletin No. 539 United States Department of Agriculture National Institute of Foods and Agriculture. 2009

Shirley Camp, MS, RD

Shirley grew up on a farm in Fulton County, Illinois. She remembers watching her grandmother and mother can food and the wonderful taste of those homemade treats. She started making grape jelly and jams as a 4-H member.

Shirley is veteran educator and retired University of Illinois Extension Nutrition Educator who helped develop the canning education curriculum for Illinois and taught for almost 40 years. During the nearly 40 years that she worked for Extension, Shirley received a Masters of Extension Education degree from the University of Illinois and completed the requirements and examination to become a Registered Dietitian.

Gale R. Ammerman, PhD

Professor emeritus of food service and technology Gale R. Ammerman passed away on April 21, 2009. Ammerman had a long career with Mississippi State University as a professor of food service and technology and as the first head of the Food Science and Human Nutrition Department. He held a doctorate from Purdue University where he was an Extension Food Technologist and Assistant Professor of Food Science. Before moving to Mississippi State he held several fruit and vegetable research positions with Libby, McNeil and Libby. He also served on technical committees of the National Research Council, National Academy of Sciences. He was a Fellow of the Institute of Food Technologists and served as president of the Council for Agricultural Science and Technology.

INTRODUCTION

Yes, there really was a Mrs. Wages

...a feisty lady who loved to put up food from her garden. She and her husband had a country store near Tupelo, Mississippi, back in the early '50s, that was a gathering spot for local farmers. It was an old-fashioned store where folks came for everything from horse harnesses to ice cream...and the latest gossip.

Then, in the late '60s, a friend, Mr. Erskin Dacus of Dacus Drug Co., dropped by the store. He was looking for a good pickling lime recipe to add to a line of home canning products he was putting together and was overheard by shoppers, who immediately recommended Mrs. Wages' recipe. And the rest is history: Dacus tried Mrs. Wages' recipe and bought it on the spot, and the Mrs. Wages family recipe became an instant hit.

And while Mrs. Wages has passed away, her line of home canning products is still around...and still produced with the same fussy commitment to quality and wholesomeness that made it a favorite 50 years ago. Better still, it is available nationwide and includes a full array of products for pickling, canning, jelly making, preserving fruit, and more.

What's more, Mrs. Wages remains as committed to quality and to home canning as ever.

Home Canning Today

Many households find home canning is a practical and enjoyable way to preserve garden produce at its finest. Almost every vegetable and fruit may be canned and their goodness and flavor saved for those nutritious, delicious meals in the winter.

If you're the wondering, worrying kind, you'll appreciate home canning. You won't be wondering what additives, what chemical preservatives, or how much sugar and salt are in those cans of food as you open them. You'll know exactly how much, if any, sugar and salt you've added, and there's no reason to add chemical preservatives.

And if you need another good reason for home canning, make it deep satisfaction. That's what you'll feel when you've completed your canning and you look with admiration at those quart jars of tomatoes ready for pasta sauce, or salsa, beans, corn, beets, and carrots, jars of so many varieties of pickles, jams, jellies, and preserves, apple pie filling, spiced apples and so much more.

But is home canning safe?

Unequivocally, yes. If you follow these directions carefully, there's no reason to fear the results.

Canning was risky back in grandma's day. She used old containers, rubber rings that often didn't seal properly, and did it all in a big boiler, just as her mother had taught her.

Today, equipment is far better. More importantly, commercial firms and the U.S. Department of Agriculture and the National Institute of Food and Agriculture have joined in studies of canning safety. Canning methods have been tested, retested, and tested again.

Grandma's ways have been discarded in favor of methods that are easier, quicker, far safer, and that preserve more of the goodness of fruits and vegetables.

Don't let the lack of an orchard or vegetable garden stop you from canning. There are fruit and vegetables aplenty at farmers' markets, pick-your-own places, and grocery stores. Choose the freshest produce at their peak of ripeness, and process them as quickly as possible.

You'll find home canning is enjoyable and satisfying, and the results are food that is nutritious and top quality.

THE BASICS OF CANNING

You'll discover that canning is just as easy and just as rewarding as cooking. However, there is a difference and it is important. When you cook, you may follow a recipe. At times, you adjust it to your own tastes or those of your family. You leave out that much garlic in the stew; add nuts to that whole wheat bread recipe. You change the ingredients a bit, to make the recipe truly yours.

You cannot do this when you're canning. Experimenting can be dangerous. Time and temperatures have been researched very carefully for canning. Too little time or too low a temperature means you're not protecting the food against bacteria, enzymes, molds, and yeasts.

Too much time or too high temperatures may mean you're needlessly destroying nutrients in the food, and damaging its taste. Follow the directions exactly as stated in the recipe.

Let's start with the basics.

CANNING METHODS

Acidity

The amount and method of heat processing used depends mainly on the acidity in food. Acidity may be natural, as in most fruits, or added, as in pickled food. Low-acid canned foods contain too little acidity to prevent the growth of heat-resistant bacteria. Acid foods contain enough acidity to block their growth or destroy them more rapidly when heated.

The term *pH* is a measure of acidity; the lower its value, the more acid the food. The acidity level in foods can be increased by adding vinegar, lemon juice, or Mrs. Wages® Citric Acid. Consumers cannot accurately measure the pH of food at home.

Acid foods have a pH of 4.6 or lower. They include fruits, pickles, sauerkraut, jams, jellies, marmalades, and fruit butters. Although tomatoes usually are considered an acid food, some have pH values slightly above 4.6, therefore, if they are to be canned as acid foods, tomatoes must be acidified to a pH or 4.6 or lower with lemon juice or Mrs. Wages® Citric Acid prior to processing. Figs and Asian pears are also acidified before processing in a boiling water bath canner.

Tomatoes, figs, and Asian pears have pH values of 4.0 to 4.6 after lemon juice or Mrs. Wages® Citric Acid is added. Their final acidity allows the growth of some mildly heat-resistant, spore-forming bacteria. A 45- to 85-minute process time in boiling water is needed to achieve a high enough temperature to destroy bacteria and to ensure the safe-keeping of canned tomatoes, figs, and Asian pears.

Jams, jellies, conserves, apple and grape juices, and some pickled products are higher in acid and have pH values around 3.0. These high acid foods have a 5 to 15-minute processing time in a boiling water bath canner.

Most berry fruits, apples, apricots, grapes, nectarines, peaches, pears, pineapples, some pickled foods, and rhubarb have pH values of 3.4 to 4.0, and require a longer processing time to destroy their native spoilage microorganisms. These foods are processed in a boiling water bath canner from 10 to 30 minutes.

Low-acid foods have pH values higher than 4.6. Meats, poultry, fish, seafood, milk and all fresh vegetables except for most tomatoes are low-acid foods with pH values above 4.6. Their natural acid level is too low to prevent the growth of the heat-resistant spore-forming bacteria common on these foods. These foods must, therefore, be canned in a pressure canner to be safe. Most mixtures of low-acid and acid foods also have pH values above 4.6 unless their recipes include enough vinegar or lemon juice to make them acid foods. These mixtures must also be processed in a pressure canner.

Boiling water bath method

This is used for acid foods. These include all fruits, tomatoes, sauerkraut, jams, jellies, preserves, and most foods to which vinegar has been added, such as most pickles and relishes.

Pressure canner method

This method is used for foods containing little acid. These include vegetables (except for tomatoes), meats, seafood, and mixtures of food that include some low-acid foods.

All foods, acid and non-acid, contain enzymes that can harbor growth of molds and yeasts, which will cause food to spoil. Molds and yeasts may be inactivated or destroyed by heat through either boiling water bath or pressure canning method.

The pressure canner method is used to destroy other food-bacteria and their byproducts in home canned foods. These include *Salmonella, Staphylococcus aureus,* and *Clostridium botulinum*, the cause of botulism.

Since these harmful bacteria are not a problem in high-acid foods, there's no reason to use this high temperature method with them. These bacteria will thrive in low-acid foods and are not destroyed by the 212°F temperature of the boiling water bath method, but are destroyed by processing at 240°F for a specific amount of time. This heat is only achievable at home through the pressure canner method.

PACKING METHODS

Raw Pack or Cold Pack

These terms, used interchangeably, refer to putting uncooked food into a heated jar to which a hot liquid is added.

Hot Pack

This refers to putting food that has been cooked to some degree into jars for processing. Hot pack sometimes requires less processing time, since the food is partially cooked. Sometimes it takes as long, or longer, because of the denser pack. Hot packing is often preferred because it softens the food and allows the food to be packed more easily.

Instructions for each food will explain which of these packing methods should be used, and the processing time required.

Headspace

When packing prepared fruit or vegetables into jars, a certain amount of head space must allowed. Headspace is the space between the top of the produce and liquid and the rim of the jar. It allows the food to expand during the canning process and is essential if a vacuum is to be created. The amount of headspace is specific to each type of food being preserved. If too much headspace is left, the jar may not seal properly because all the air may not be driven out of the jar. If too little headspace is left, the food may bubble out during processing leaving a deposit on the lid which may interfere with the seal.

TIPS FOR FIRST-TIME CANNERS

If this is your first attempt at canning, here are some hints that should make it easier for you:

- Begin with a clean, sanitary kitchen.

- Start small. Six quarts of tomatoes or six jars of jam or jelly are plenty for this first try.

- Be prepared with everything you need:
    - o Jars and new lids
    - o Canner(s) including a pressure (dial or weighted gauge) canner; (remember a dial-type gauge must be tested annually); and a water bath canner with a rack
    - o Jar lifter
    - o Spoons and other utensils
    - o Plastic bubbler or narrow spatula to remove air bubbles from filled jars
    - o Clean cloth towels

- Fresh, ripe produce that's at the peak of perfection and free from defects.

- A large cleared area to work in. Canning takes lots of space.

- Allow more time than you think you will need. Believe you should have it done in an hour? Give yourself two hours and feel no pressure.

- Have patience and give yourself time to learn. Realize that canning is a lot like many other kitchen tasks, it gets a lot easier the second time you do it.

THE EQUIPMENT YOU'LL NEED

Here are two rules regarding equipment:

1. Make certain equipment is in good condition. A pressure canner with a faulty gauge or jars with nicked edges can cause food to spoil.

2. Make certain equipment is available and within reach. Lay out all needed equipment in the kitchen before you start. Mid-point in a canning session is not the time to remember you forgot to buy canning lids.

Canners

You'll need a pressure canner if you can vegetables (except for tomatoes, sauerkraut, and pickles), meats, or mixtures of low-acid foods, plus a kettle or large stock pot with a cover and rack if you're canning fruits, jams, jellies, pickles, etc. using the boiling water bath method.

Pressure canners are manufactured in various sizes; match your canner with your canning ambitions, if you will do a lot of canning, buy a big canner and save both time and heating costs with it. When using a pressure canner, follow the manufacturer's instructions. All canners require a rack on the bottom, so boiling water can circulate under the jars.

The *dial-type* pressure canner has a gauge that shows the pressure, a petcock that allows steam to escape under a controlled pressure, and a safety valve that will pop and thus relieve pressure if the petcock becomes stuck. The dial-type gauge must be checked for accuracy each year. This service may be provided by your State Extension Service or at stores where canners are sold. If the dial is inaccurate either way by two or more pounds, you need to replace the gauge.

The *weighted-gauge pressure canner* has a metal weight-type pressure control. When the desired pressure is reached, you will hear the control jiggle, releasing steam and preventing the pressure from rising higher. The weight on this type of canner may be set at 5, 10, 15, or 20 pounds. This type of canner does not need to be tested for accuracy.

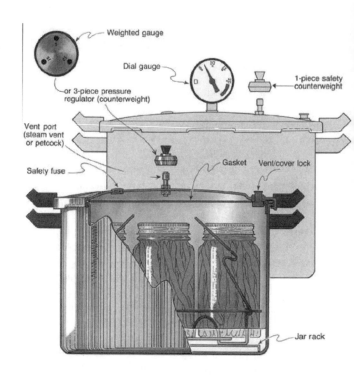

Weighted gauge

Dial gauge

1-piece safety counterweight

or 3-piece pressure regulator (counterweight)

Vent port (steam vent or petcock)

Safety fuse

Gasket   Vent/cover lock

Jar rack

Source: USDA Complete Guide to Home Canning, National Institute of Food and Agriculture, Agriculture Information Bulletin No. 539, 2009.

A *kettle or large stock pot* with a rack and cover is used for boiling water bath canning of high-acid foods. Most people use a conventional black enamel canner although stainless steel canners are available as well. It is resistant to acids and salt solutions, so it can double for cooking pickles or brining vegetables. The kettle must be deep enough so jars sitting on a rack will be covered with at least one inch of water. There must be at least another inch in the kettle for the space required for a rolling boil. A pressure canner may be used for boiling water bath canning, too. Set it so that no pressure builds up inside by not locking the lid in place. Leave the petcock open or remove the weighted gauge so that steam can easily escape.

JARS AND LIDS

Jars are sold in sizes from 4 ounces to a half-gallon, and with two-piece lids. Most popular are pint and quart sizes with a *vacuum-seal lid* held in place during processing by a metal band. The underside of the lid (also referred to as a "flat") has a strip of rubberlike sealing compound on the edge, where it comes in contact with the rim of the jar. A metal screw band holds the lid in place during processing and is removed when the jar has cooled and the jar has been sealed. With these lids, it's easy to tell when the seal is perfect. The lid makes a definite snapping click or ping when it seals while cooling. The lid curves downward when sealed and remains so. When tapped with a spoon, the sealed lid rings clear. These lids are discarded after one use; the bands are saved.

Before beginning any canning recipe, prepare jars and lids as directed by manufacturer. Keep jars hot until ready to fill.

While we think all glass jars are created equal, we do not recommend using commercial one-time jars that may have held foods such as pickles or pasta sauce. Also, colored glass canning jars that are blue, green, or brown are antiques and should only be used for decorative purposes. You may still find jars with glass lids and clamps and other decorator-type jars available, we recommend using these for storage and decoration, not for canning.

Household utensils and equipment

These include knives, long-handled spoons, saucepans, measuring cups, a colander, scrapers and plenty of hand towels. Always use *non-reactive pots* and *pans* when canning. Never use aluminum pots or pans.

Additional Aids

The *jar lifter* is used for removing jars from the canner. Use one and you won't burn your hands.

The *jar funnel* with its wide mouth makes it easy to fill jars without getting the food on the rim of the jars.

A *bubble freer or bubbler* is handy and inexpensive, and makes it easy to get bubbles out of the food before processing. Many bubblers also act as a headspace measuring tool.

A *lid lifter* is a small wand with a magnet on one end that aids in removing hot lids from water.

A *kitchen timer* is needed to accurately keep processing times.

Use a *kitchen scale* to accurately measure your produce.

A pair of food-safe *plastic gloves* is recommended if handling any type of hot pepper to protect your skin from irritation.

If your plans include making jelly, you will need a *jelly bag* or *cheesecloth* to strain the fruit.

Capacities of Canners

	½ Pints	Pints	Quarts	½ Gallons
4 Quart*	4	4		
6 Quart	7	7		
8 Quart	14**	7	4	
16 Quart	20**	9	7	
21 Quart		18**	7	4***

SELECTING PRODUCE

The fruits and vegetables you preserve should be prizewinners, at the very peak of perfection, and certainly not too ripe and with no blemishes or bruises. Whether from your garden, a grocery store, or produce market, produce should be fresh. Ideally, you will both pick or buy and can on the same day. If that's impossible, produce should be refrigerated.

Wash the produce carefully and completely, then pare or cut up with clean knives.

Here are some suggestions on a few of the vegetables and fruits you may be canning:

Beets - Usually best when no more than two to three inches in diameter. Some varieties stay tender and flavorful when larger and may be canned.

Lima Beans - Best when pods are well filled and the seed is firm but not hard.

Snap Beans - Harvest when so crisp that they snap readily.

Corn - Try to complete canning within four hours of picking before sugar is converted to starch. Kernels should be plump, milky, and bright. If immature, corn will be watery and tasteless. If too mature, corn will be starchy and tasteless.

Greens - Use young, tender leaves of mustard, spinach, kale, and collard greens. Kale is better if harvested after a frost.

Okra - Pick pods when two to three inches long.

Peas - Pick as soon as they are mature enough to be shelled.

Tomatoes - Select tomatoes that are firm and ripe but not overripe. They should be free of bruises, spots, decay, molds, cracks and growths. Otherwise tomatoes may be low in acid—too low for safe canning. If picking from your own garden, be sure to use tomatoes from plants that are disease free.

Apples - If canning slices, remember that green apples with seeds not yet brown, will produce hard, sour slices. Overripe fruit will be mushy, looking much like applesauce. The best applesauce is made by blending two or more cooking-type apple varieties. Green apples make sour sauce; overripe apples make a watery, bland sauce.

Berries - Harvest blackberries, raspberries, dewberries, bramble berries and similar fruits in shallow trays or pans, to avoid crushing the berries. Can the day of picking. If that's impossible, quickly cool the berries to 33°-35°F. and hold overnight at that temperature.

Cherries - Pick when red-ripe, sound, and not over-soft. Hold at 33°-35°F. temperature if canning is delayed more than four hours after picking.

Gooseberries - Pick when most of the berries are full-sized but still green or showing only the first blush of color. If holding them overnight, keep them at about 40°F.

Pears - Unlike most fruits, pears should not be ripened on the tree. If they are, they begin to rot inside, and will quickly spoil. Pick when full-sized, mature green, and when they can be picked easily from the tree. Pick and handle carefully, to avoid bruises, since damaged fruit will spoil quickly. Store pears until ripe in a cool place that is free of odors. This may take a few days or weeks, depending on the variety.

Plums - Should be tree-ripened for best flavor, with deep color and a powdery bloom. Can quickly, if possible, since they become mushy very rapidly.

YIELD FROM
FRESH VEGETABLES AND FRUITS

The number of quarts of canned food you get from a given amount of fresh vegetables and fruits depends on quality, condition, maturity and variety, as well as the size of the pieces and how the fruit or vegetable is packed.

Generally, the following amounts make one quart of canned food:

Vegetable	Pounds
Asparagus	2½ - 4½
Beans, lima, in pods	3 - 5
Beans, snap	1½ - 2½
Beets, without tops	2 - 3½
Carrots, without tops	2 - 3
Corn, sweet, in husks	3 - 6
Cucumbers, pickling	1 - 2
Okra	1½
Peas, green, in pods	3 - 6
Pumpkin or winter squash	1½ - 3
Spinach and other greens	2 - 6
Squash, summer	2 - 4
Sweet potatoes	2 - 3
Tomatoes	3

Fruit	Pounds
Apples	2½ - 3
Applesauce	2½ - 3½
Apricots	2 - 2½
Berries	1½ - 3
Cherries	2 - 2½
Peaches	2 - 3
Pears	2 - 3
Plums	1½ - 2½

Before you Begin:

Here's a checklist before you begin canning:

1. Check all jars. Are they all free of cracks or nicks on the rims? Any other damage, so they shouldn't be used? Do you have enough jars?

2. Check the lids and rings. Do you have enough? Are the vacuum lids new and rust-free? Are the screw bands rust-free?

3. Is your canning equipment clean?

4. If you're using a dial-gauge pressure canner, has the gauge been checked this year?

5. Do you have all the other equipment you'll need?

6. Have you washed the jars with detergent and then rinsed them? (And if you washed them in the dishwasher, just leave them in there until you're ready to use them. They'll stay hot.)

7. Are the jars sitting now in clean, hot water, ready for use?

8. Are the lids and bands clean? (Follow the lid manufacturer's instructions. Those instructions may call for keeping the lids in hot water until used.)

9. Have blemishes been removed from the produce, so it is ready for canning? And has it been scrubbed clean?

BOILING WATER BATH CANNING

This method of canning is easy and popular. It should be used only for high-acid foods. These include fruits, tomatoes, and some foods with vinegar added. It can be used with both raw or cold pack and hot pack method of filling the jars. In the chapters on canning specific produce, we will recommend which method to use.

You'll need a boiling water bath canner. This is a big kettle or stock pot with a tight-fitting cover. The canner also has either a metal basket or rack. This basket or rack holds the jars off the bottom of the kettle so that hot water can circulate underneath. The rack also keeps the jars separate from each other, and has handles so that all the jars in the kettle can be lifted in or out at the same time.

The kettle must be deep enough so that the jar tops are covered by one inch of boiling water, with at least an additional inch or two of space above the water. Most quart jars are 7 to 7½ inches tall, so a canner should be 12 or more inches deep.

This same kettle can be used in making jams, preserves, and marmalade.

STEP BY STEP INSTRUCTIONS FOR BOILING WATER BATH CANNING:

1. Before beginning any canning recipe, prepare jars and lids as directed by manufacturer. Keep jars hot until ready to fill.

2. Fill the canner half full of water, place it on the stove, and begin simmering. Heat another small kettle of water.

3. Place raw or hot-packed food in the clean, hot jars, leaving the recommended head space.

4. Add salt if desired. *Salt is not necessary for preservation.* If you use salt, use Mrs. Wages® Pickling & Canning Salt which does not contain additives that will make the liquid cloudy.

5. Run a plastic bubble freer (much better than a table knife or spatula, although a narrow spatula may used) around the inside of the jars to release any air bubbles.

6. Wipe the top of each jar with a damp cloth or paper towel if your syrup contains sugar, or with a dry towel if not. Do this thoroughly and carefully to prevent small particles of food from interfering with the seal.

7. Center the lid over the mouth of each jar. Screw the band down firmly to finger-tight. Do not over-tighten the bands as this may damage the rings and/or not allow air to escape during processing.

8. Lower the jars into the boiling water canner with a jar lifter. Make sure jars are not touching to get good heat circulation. A wire basket or rack will keep the jars properly spaced.

9. Add boiling water from the other kettle to cover the jars by one or two inches.

10. Put canner lid on, turn heat up, and start timing when water is at full boil.

11. When the recommended time is up, remove the canner from the heat and remove the lid. Leave jars in the canner undisturbed for five minutes. This added time completes the processing and helps create a better seal. Remove the jars with a lifter or by lifting out the basket. Lift jars straight out of the canner without tilting. *Do not leave the jars in the canner overnight — this can result in an unsafe product.*

12. Put the jars on a cake rack or towel in a draft-free area. Don't knock them together; they will shatter easily when hot. Leave about an inch of space between jars so they can cool adequately. Do not cover them and keep them out of drafts. *Do not turn the jars upside down.*

13. Do not tighten or loosen the screw bands. Leave jars undisturbed for 12 to 24 hours to cool.

14. Test the seal by pressing on the lid or tapping it with a spoon. A sealed lid will not give and will have a hollow sound when tapped. If the seal is not good, you can reprocess the jars within twenty-four hours of the original processing. Be sure to use new lids. However, to eliminate over-cooking which results in loss of nutrients and quality, we recommend immediate refrigeration and early use, or freezing the product instead of reprocessing. Try to discover why your jars didn't seal. The most common reasons are a bit of food caught between the lid and the jar rim, and cracks or nicks on the jar rim.

15. Remove the screw bands from the jars.

16. Wipe the jars clean and label them with the produce name, its origin, and the date. This is helpful when you're planning next year.

17. Store the jars in a cool, dry, dark place. Dampness rusts the lids and causes the seals to deteriorate. Light tends to destroy vitamins and fade colors. Freezing and thawing will ruin the food's taste and possibly break the seal.

Plan to eat canned foods within one year. While the food may be safe to eat for much longer, there's no reason to settle for old canned goods when next year's harvest will supply good fresh produce.

Boil all home canned vegetables in a covered saucepan at a full rolling boil for 10 minutes before serving. Home canned spinach or corn should be boiled for 20 minutes. If the food looks spoiled, foams or has an off odor during heating, destroy it. Do not taste it!

Altitude Adjustments

Processing times listed in Mrs. Wages® Home Canning Guide are based on altitudes less than 1,000 feet below sea level, unless noted. Because water boils at lower temperatures as altitudes rise, it's necessary to allow more time during processing. The USDA recommends increasing processing time by 1 minute for every 1000 feet of altitude for those items processed 20 minutes or less. For those products processed for more than 20 minutes, it is recommended to increase the processing time by 2 minutes for every 1000 feet of altitude.

PRESSURE CANNING

STEP BY STEP INSTRUCTIONS

1. Before beginning any canning recipe, prepare jars and lids as directed by manufacturer. Keep jars hot until ready to fill.

2. Place basket or rack in canner. For foods canned by the hot pack method, put boiling water into the canner. See accompanying table for exact amount. Set canner on low heat. For foods canned by the raw pack method, put the same amount of hot, but not boiling, water into the canner. Set on low heat but do not allow water to reach simmering temperature.

3. Place raw or hot-packed food in clean, hot jars, leaving the recommended headspace. Add salt if desired. *Salt is not necessary for preservation.*

4. Run a plastic bubble freer (much better than a table knife or spatula, although a narrow spatula will work) around the inside edge of the jars to release any air bubbles. Adjust lids just to finger tight. Do not over-tighten rings as this could damage the rings and not allow air to escape from jar.

5. Place each prepared jar upright into canner on the rack or basket. Jars must not be touching each other or the bottom of the canner so steam can circulate freely.

6. Place the cover on the canner and lock it securely.

7. Set the burner to the highest heat. Set controls so that steam can flow freely from the canner. Allow steam to vent vigorously for ten minutes from canner.

8. Halt flow of steam by placing the pressure regulator on the vent pipe of weighted gauge canners or closing the control valve by turning the valve stem down to the horizontal position or by placing the counterweight on the vent pipe in weighted gauge canners.

9. Allow the pressure to build up to ten pounds for canning at 240° F. Watch the gauge closely on dial gauge canners and when the dial is almost at ten pounds, turn the heat down to low. With weighted gauge canners, reduce the heat when the gauge begins to jiggle vigorously. The heat should be high enough to make the gauge jiggle two or three times a minute.

10. Check the dial-type gauge or the weighted gauge to maintain the correct pressure in the canner. Avoid rapid temperature changes during processing that may cause varying pressures and force liquid from the jars.

11. Start counting the processing time as soon as the required pressure is reached.

12. As soon as the processing time is up, remove canner from heat or turn burner to off. Allow the pressure to return to zero gradually. Keep in mind that in many canners, the cooling process will take the same amount of time or longer than the canning process. Do not run cold water over the canner, remove the pressure regulator, or open the control valve to speed the cooling process. With dial-gauge canners, when the dial reaches zero, remove

the pressure regulator or open the control valve very slowly. With weight control canners, check to see if the pressure has returned to zero by lifting the control slightly with a fork. If steam spurts out, the pressure is still up, so wait a little longer. If you do not see steam, remove the control.

13. Once the pressure is at zero, wait 10 minutes before opening the canner. This allows for the canning process to complete the seal. Release the cover from the locked position and remove it, lifting the far edge first, so that you shield yourself from the steam.

14. Remove jars from the canner without tilting the jars and set on a rack or towel to cool. Do not tighten the screw bands. Leave an inch of space around jars and do not place them in a drafty area. Keep the jars uncovered and allow them to cool completely and undisturbed.

15. When the jars are cool, test the seal. A sealed lid will not give when pressing down and will sound hollow when tapped with a spoon. If it has not sealed, you may reprocess the jars within twenty-four hours of the original processing, and follow original instructions for canning. Be sure to use new lids.

16. Remove the screw bands from the jars.

17. Wipe the jars clean and label them with the produce name, the origin, and the date.

18. Store the jars in a cool, dry, dark place.

Water Needs

Follow manufacturer's instructions, if different from these recommendations.

Size of Canner (Quarts)	Amount of Water for Processing (Quarts)
4	1
6	1½
8	1½
16	2
21	2

Altitude Adjustments

At altitudes above sea level, adjustment of the amount of pressure needed for safe food processing must be made in order for the canner to reach the desired temperature of 240°F.

When using a Weight Control Canner in altitudes of 2,000 feet or greater, use 15 pounds of pressure. For Dial Gauge Canners, use this table as a guideline.

Altitude	Pounds Pressure for Canning Low-Acid Vegetables
Up to 1,000 feet	10
1,001 - 2,000	11
2,001 - 4,000	12
4,001 - 6,000	13
6,001 - 8,000	14
8,001 - 10,000	15

Successful Pressure Canning Tips

1. Read carefully and follow the instructions that came with your pressure canner.

2. Keep the pressure canner clean and in good working order. Clean all openings with a string, pipe cleaner, toothpick, or tiny brush to remove any food particles that might hamper the flow of air and steam. Do this before you use the canner.

3. Prepare only enough fruits and vegetables for one canner load of jars at a time.

4. Fill jars quickly, so they won't cool on your table or counter. Use a wide-mouth funnel and avoid spilling liquid on the rim of the jar, where it may interfere with a good seal.

5. Measure headspace carefully when filling jars.

6. When removing bubbles, avoid stirring jar contents and thus adding more air.

7. If you use salt, up to 1 teaspoon per quart may be added just before you cap the jars. Use Mrs. Wages® Pickling & Canning Salt to prevent cloudy liquid.

8. Do not leave the kitchen while the food is being processed. It's imperative that the pressure be maintained at all times.

9. Some pressure canners have a second locking system that prevents them from being opened while there is still pressure inside. If you are buying a canner, this is a desirable feature.

CONSUMING HOME CANNED GOODS

Plan to eat canned foods within one year. While the food may be safe to eat for much longer, there's no reason to settle for old canned goods when next year's harvest will supply good fresh produce.

Boil all home canned vegetables in a covered saucepan at a full rolling boil for 10 minutes before serving. Home canned spinach or corn should be boiled for 20 minutes. If the food looks spoiled, foams or has an off odor during heating, destroy it. Do not taste it! When in doubt, throw it out!

REMEDIES FOR CANNING PROBLEMS

Fruits & Vegetables

Problem	Cause(s)	Prevention
Loss of liquid from glass jars during processing (not a sign of spoilage). (Do not open to replace liquid.)	1. Lowering pressure in canner suddenly after processing period.	1. Do not force pressure down by placing canner in a draft, opening the petcock too soon, etc. Allow pressure to drop to zero naturally; wait 10 minutes before opening.
	2. Fluctuating pressure during processing in pressure canner.	2. Maintain a constant temperature throughout processing time.
	3. Failure to work out air bubbles from jars before processing.	3. Remove by running a bubble freer between food and jar.
	4. Improper seal.	4. Follow the manufacturer's directions for closure used.
	5. Jars not covered with water in water bath canner.	5. Jars should be covered with 1 to 2 inches of water in canner throughout processing period. If water falls below 1-inch or stops boiling, add more boiling water and restart the timing process.
	6. Starchy foods absorbed liquid.	6. None.
	7. Insufficient headspace.	7. Measure headspace carefully and follow recommended headspace.
Imperfect Seal (discard food unless the problem was detected within a 24 hours of processing)	1. Chips or cracks in jars.	1. Examine carefully by rubbing finger around mouth of the jar.
	2. Failure to follow recommended directions for lids.	2. Follow manufacturer's directions.
	3. Particles left on mouth of jar.	3. Use a clean, damp cloth or paper towel to clean rim of jar in order to remove any particles that would prevent a good seal.
	4. Using old closures that should be discarded.	4. Do not reuse self-sealing metal lids or rusty bands.

Fruits & Vegetables continued

Problem	Cause(s)	Prevention
Imperfect Seal (discard food unless the problem was detected within a 24 hours of processing)	5. Lifting jars by tops or inverting while hot.	5. Use jar lifter for removing jars from canner or grasp below lip. Leave in upright position.
Product dark at top of jar (not necessarily a sign of spoilage).	1. Air left in the jars permits oxidation.	1. Remove air bubbles before sealing jars. Use recommended headspace.
	2. Insufficient amount of liquid or syrup.	2. Cover product with water or syrup.
	3. Food not processed long enough to destroy enzymes.	3. Process recommended length of time.
Cloudy liquid (sometimes denotes spoilage).	1. Starch in vegetables.	1. Select products at desirable state of maturity. Do not use over-mature vegetables.
	2. Minerals in water.	2. Use soft water.
	3. Fillers in table salt.	3. Use pure refined salt, such as Mrs. Wages® Pickling & Canning Salt.
	4. Spoilage.	4. Process by recommended method and for recommended time.
Color changes that are undesirable.	1. Contact with minerals such as iron, zinc, or copper in cooking utensils or water.	1. Avoid these conditions by using carefully selected cooking utensils. Use soft water.
	2. Over-processing.	2. Follow directions for processing time.
	3. Immature or over-mature product.	3. Select fruits and vegetable at optimum stage of maturity.
	4. Exposure to light.	4. Best to store canned foods in a dark place.
	5. May be a distinct spoilage.	5. If any "off" odor or spoilage is suspected discard food and sterilize or destroy jar.
	6. Natural and harmless substances in fruits and vegetables.	6. None.
Floating (especially some fruits)	1. Over-processing fruits and tomatoes destroys pectin.	1. Follow directions for processing time.
	2. Fruit is lighter than syrup.	2. Use firm, ripe fruit. Heat before packing. Use light to medium syrup.
	3. Improper packing.	3. Pack fruit as closely as possible without crushing it.

continued on next page

Fruits & Vegetables continued

Problem	Cause(s)	Prevention
Spoilage	1. Incorrect pressure.	1. Gauge should be checked every year for accuracy.
	2. Over-packing.	2. Jars should be well filled, but not packed.
	3. Incorrect timing.	3. Follow directions for timing.
	4. Incorrect method used.	4. Low-acid vegetables and meats must be pressure canned for safety.
	5. Poor selection of fruits and vegetables.	5. Select produce of suitable variety and at proper stage of maturity. Preserve immediately after gathering.

Juices

Problem	Cause(s)	Prevention
Fermentation or spoilage	1. Failure to process adequately.	1. Juices should be processed in boiling water bath (212°F).
	2. Imperfect seal.	2. Use recommended methods and processing times. Use perfect jars and new lids. Wipe rim of jar clean of any spills from filling before placing lid and securing band.
	3. Air left in jars.	3. Proper processing will exhaust air from jars.
Cloudy sediment in bottom of jar	1. Solids in juice settle.	1. Juice may be restrained and made into jelly. Shake juices if used as a beverage.
Separation of juice (usually found in tomato juice)	1. Enzymatic change during handling after cutting.	1. Heat tomatoes quickly to simmering temperature.
Poor flavor	1. Immature, over-ripe, or inferior fruit used.	1. Use only good-quality, firm, ripe fruit or tomatoes for making juice.
	2. Use of too much water for extracting juice.	2. Use only amount of water called for in directions. No water is added to tomatoes.
	3. Improper storage.	3. Cool, dark, dry storage.

Home Canning

GUIDE AND RECIPES

TOMATOES

CANNING TOMATOES

Selecting Tomatoes

Carefully select tomatoes. They should be ripe and juicy, but not overripe and with no decayed or soft areas. A single poor tomato can spoil a batch. Discard overripe tomatoes and those with any bad spots. Choose tomatoes from plants that are healthy and disease free. Tomatillos may be canned using tomato canning procedures.

Acidification

Regardless of what variety of tomatoes you are using, current recommendations are to acidify all tomato products. To ensure safe acidity in whole, crushed, or juiced tomatoes, for pints, add ¼ teaspoon Mrs. Wages® Citric Acid or add 1 tablespoon of bottled lemon juice directly to each pint jar. For quarts, add ½ teaspoon of Mrs. Wages® Citric Acid or add 2 tablespoons of bottled lemon juice directly to each quart jar.

To be sure you acidify each jar of canned product, measure the lemon juice or Mrs. Wages® Citric Acid into the empty jars before you fill them. Please note, using 4 tablespoons of 5% acidity vinegar per quart or 2 tablespoons per pint will also acidify tomatoes, however, vinegar may cause unwanted flavor changes.

Preparing Tomatoes

Most canning recipes involving tomatoes require you to blanch, peel, and core tomatoes. To do so, simply prepare a stockpot of boiling water. Thoroughly wash tomatoes and remove stems. Dip a few tomatoes at a time in this boiling water for 30 seconds or until skins start to split, and then put them in cold water. Skin tomatoes and cut out cores and any green portions. Follow the recipe instructions for further preparation.

Hot Pack Method

Tomatoes are easy to preserve, but the canning instructions should be followed carefully to assure the canned tomatoes are not only safe to eat but also tasty and at their nutritional peak. *The raw pack method for canning tomatoes is no longer recommended.*

CRUSHED TOMATOES

STEP BY STEP INSTRUCTIONS:

1. Select tomatoes for canning carefully. Discard overripe tomatoes and those with any bad spots. Choose tomatoes from plants that are healthy and disease free.

2. Wash jars in hot, soapy water, then rinse in hot water and leave in hot water until ready to use. (Or wash in dishwasher and hold to keep hot.)

3. Prepare home canning jars and lids according to manufacturer's instructions for sterilized jars.

4. Fill hot water bath canner half full of water and place over heat. Heat a kettle of water.

5. Prepare an additional saucepan of boiling water for peeling tomatoes. Dip a few tomatoes at a time in this boiling water for 30 to 60 seconds or until skins begin to split then put them in cold water. Skin tomatoes and cut out cores and any green portions. Quarter tomatoes.

6. Crush a few of the tomatoes and put them in a large pot. Bring to a boil. Add one or two tomatoes at a time, to maintain a constant temperature. Heating tomatoes this way instead of all at the same time is recommended to destroy the enzyme pectinase that causes canned tomatoes to separate in the jars.

7. Boil all tomatoes for 5 minutes.

8. For safe acidity, add ¼ teaspoon of Mrs. Wages® Citric Acid or use 1 tablespoon bottled lemon juice directly to each pint jar. For quarts, add ½ teaspoon of Mrs. Wages® Citric Acid or add 2 tablespoons of bottled lemon juice directly to each quart jar.

9. Fill hot jars with boiling tomatoes, leaving ½-inch headspace.

10. If desired for taste (it is not needed for preservation), add Mrs. Wages® Pickling & Canning Salt, ½ teaspoon per pint, or 1 teaspoon per quart.

11. Remove air bubbles with bubble freer.

12. Wipe sealing edge with a dry towel, put on lid, screw band on finger tight.

13. Lower jars onto rack in canner. Add hot water to cover the jars by one or two inches. Put on the lid, and bring water to a rolling boil.

14. Begin timing when water is at full boil. Process pints for 35 minutes, quarts for 45 minutes.

15. Remove canner from heat and remove lid. Let jars stand in water undisturbed for 5 minutes to complete the process.

16. Carefully remove jars using a jar lifter; do not tilt jar. Do not tighten bands. Set on cake rack or towel in a draft-free area. Leave jars undisturbed for 12 to 24 hours.

17. Test the seal. If dome of lid is down, the seal is good.

18. Remove the screw bands. Label jars. Store in a cool, dry, dark place.

Note:

Add Mrs. Wages® Bloody Mary drink mix seasoning to your canned tomato juice and serve. Or to make a Bloody Mary seasoned tomato juice, use the recipe on this page and in Step 4, omit salt; add Mrs. Wages Bloody Mary Seasoning Drink mix and bring juice to boil. Ladle into hot jars, leaving 1/2-inch headspace; and continue to step 5.

TOMATO JUICE

- **3-3½ pounds tomatoes per quart**
- **Mrs. Wages® Citric Acid**
- **Mrs. Wages® Pickling & Canning Salt to taste**

1. Wash tomatoes, drain, remove cores and quarter. Squeeze juice from several tomatoes into a stockpot and heat the juice. Add remainder of tomatoes. Simmer until all are soft.

2. Press cooked tomatoes through a strainer or a food mill to remove skins and seeds. Collect juice in large pot.

3. For safe acidity, add ¼ teaspoon of citric acid or use 1 tablespoon bottled lemon juice directly to each pint jar. For quarts, add ½ teaspoon of citric acid or add 2 tablespoons of bottled lemon juice directly to each quart jar.

4. Add salt, if desired. Bring juice to boil. Ladle into hot jars, leaving ½-inch headspace.

5. Wipe sealing edge with a dry towel, put on lid, screw band on finger tight. Process immediately using the boiling water bath method. Process pints for 35 minutes and quarts for 40 minutes.

6. Test jars for airtight seal 12 to 24 hours after canning. If jars are not properly sealed, refrigerate and use within a week. Label and store in a cool, dry, dark place.

WHOLE OR HALVED TOMATOES IN TOMATO JUICE

Note:
If you prefer to use a pressure canner, process pints or quarts for 25 minutes at 11 pounds pressure in a dial gauge canner or 10 pounds pressure in a weighted gauge canner.

- **3-3½ pounds tomatoes per quart**
- **Tomato Juice (enough to cover)**
- **Mrs. Wages® Citric Acid**
- **Mrs. Wages® Pickling & Canning Salt to taste**

1. Wash, peel, and core tomatoes as instructed previously. Leave whole or halve.

2. Place prepared tomatoes in large saucepan and add tomato juice until tomatoes are completely covered.

3. Bring to boil. Boil tomatoes and juice gently for 5 minutes.

4. For safe acidity, add ¼ teaspoon of citric acid or use 1 tablespoon bottled lemon juice directly to each pint jar. For quarts, add ½ teaspoon of citric acid or add 2 tablespoons of bottled lemon juice directly to each quart jar.

5. Fill hot jars with hot tomatoes, leaving ½-inch headspace. Add hot juice to jars to cover tomatoes, leaving ½-inch headspace. Remove air bubbles; wipe sealing edge with a dry towel, put on lid, screw band on finger tight.

6. Process pints and quarts in water bath canner for 85 minutes. (Longer processing time is necessary because the tomato juice used for canning is thicker and it takes longer for the heat to penetrate to the center of the jar.)

7. Test jars for airtight seal 12 to 24 hours after canning. If jars are not properly sealed, refrigerate and use within a week. Label and store in a cool, dry, dark place.

CHILI BASE

- **Approximately 6 pounds fresh, fully ripe tomatoes**
- **1 pouch Mrs. Wages® Chili Base Seasoning Mix**
- **2 tablespoons granulated sugar**

1. Wash tomatoes. Dip a few tomatoes at a time into boiling water for 30 to 60 seconds or until skins begin to split then place in cold water. Remove tomato skins. Cut in halves or quarters. Process in blender or food processor until a smooth consistency (purée) is reached.

2. Measure 5 pints (10 cups) purée into large saucepan. Add Mrs. Wages® Chili Base Seasoning Mix and sugar. Mix well.

3. Bring sauce to boil. Reduce heat to medium and simmer for 25 minutes, stirring frequently. Sauce is now ready to eat, can or freeze for future use.

4. To freeze, pour into freezer containers and let cool. Store covered in freezer up to 1 year. For canning, pour boiling hot sauce into clean, hot pint canning jars, leaving ½-inch headspace. Wipe rim clean. Adjust lids. Process for 35 minutes in boiling water bath. Boiling water should cover jars by 1-inch.

5. Test jars for airtight seal 12 to 24 hours after canning. If jars are not properly sealed, refrigerate and use within a week. Label and store in a cool, dry, dark place.

Yield: 5 pints

MRS. WAGES® CHILI RECIPE

- **1-1½ pounds ground beef**
- **1 pint prepared Mrs. Wages® Chili Base**
- **1 can (14-16 ounces) pinto beans, or kidney beans with liquid**

1. Brown ground beef. Combine beef, chili base, and pinto beans. Simmer for 20 minutes.

PIZZA SAUCE

- **Approximately 6 pounds fresh, fully ripe tomatoes**

- **1 pouch Mrs. Wages® Pizza Sauce Mix**

- **5 tablespoons granulated sugar**

1. Wash tomatoes. Dip a few tomatoes at a time into boiling water for 30 to 60 seconds or until skins begin to split. Place tomatoes in cold water. Cut out cores. Remove skins. Cut into halves or quarters. Process in blender or food processor until a smooth consistency (purée) is reached.

2. Measure 5 pints (10 cups) purée into a large saucepan. Stir in Mrs. Wages® Pizza Sauce Mix and granulated sugar. Mix well.

3. Bring sauce to boil. Reduce heat to medium and simmer for 25 minutes, stirring frequently. Sauce is now ready to eat, to can or freeze for future use.

4. To freeze, pour into freezer containers and let cool. Store covered in freezer up to 1 year. For canning, pour boiling hot sauce into clean, hot pint canning jars, leaving ½-inch headspace. Wipe rim clean and adjust lids. Process for 40 minutes in boiling water bath. Boiling water should cover jars by 1-inch.

5. Test jars for airtight seal 12 to 24 hours after canning. If jars are not properly sealed, refrigerate and use within a week. Label and store in cool, dry, dark place.

Yield: 5 pints

Note:

To use sauce: One pint of this sauce will generously cover 2 (12-inch) pizzas.

Note:

If fresh tomatoes are not available, use home or commercially canned tomatoes. Blend tomatoes and liquid from 5 pints of home-canned tomatoes, or 5 cans (1-pound each) commercially canned tomatoes into a smooth purée. The purée may also be made with 4 cans (6-ounces each) tomato paste mixed with 7 cups of water.

PASTA SAUCE

- **Approximately 6 pounds fresh, ripe tomatoes**
- **1 pouch Mrs. Wages® Pasta Sauce Mix**
- **¼ cup granulated sugar**

1. Wash tomatoes. Dip a few tomatoes at a time into boiling water for 30 to 60 seconds or until skins begin to split. Place tomatoes in cold water. Cut out cores. Remove skins. Cut in halves or quarters. Process in blender or food processor until smooth consistency (purée) is reached.

2. Pour purée into 5-quart saucepan. Stir in Mrs. Wages® Pasta Sauce Mix and sugar. Mix well.

3. Bring sauce to boil. Reduce heat to medium and simmer for 25 minutes, stirring frequently. Sauce is ready to eat, to can or freeze.

4. To freeze, pour into freezer containers and let cool. Store covered in freezer up to 1 year. To can, pour boiling hot sauce into clean, hot pint canning jars leaving ½-inch headspace. Wipe rim clean and adjust lids. Process for 40 minutes in boiling water bath. Boiling water should cover jars by 1-inch.

5. Test jars for airtight seal 12 to 24 hours after canning. If jars are not properly sealed, refrigerate and use within a week. Label and store in a cool, dry, dark place.

Yield: 5 pints

MILD, MEDIUM, OR HOT SALSA

Note:
If fresh tomatoes are not available, use home-canned or commercially canned tomatoes. If using canned tomatoes, do not drain liquid

- Approximately 6 pounds fresh tomatoes
- 1 pouch (4-ounce) Mrs. Wages® Salsa Mix (Mild, Medium, or Hot variety)
- ½ cup Mrs. Wages® Pickling & Canning Vinegar or other commercial white vinegar (5% acidity)

1. Wash tomatoes. Dip a few tomatoes at a time into boiling water for 30 to 60 seconds or until skins begin to split. Place tomatoes in cold water. Cut out cores. Remove skins. Coarsely chop tomatoes.

2. Measure 5 pints (10 cups) chopped tomatoes into 5 quart saucepan. Stir in Mrs. Wages® Salsa Mix and vinegar. Mix well.

3. Bring salsa to boil, stirring occasionally. Reduce heat and simmer for 10 minutes, stirring occasionally. Salsa is ready to eat, can or freeze.

4. To freeze, pour into freezer containers and let cool. Store covered in freezer up to 1 year. To can, pour hot salsa into clean, hot pint canning jars leaving ½-inch headspace. Wipe rim clean and adjust lids. Process for 40 minutes in boiling water bath. Boiling water should cover jars by 1-inch.

5. Test jars for airtight seal 12 to 24 hours after canning. If jars are not properly sealed, refrigerate and use within a week. Label and store in a cool, dry, dark place.

Yield: 5 pints

Note:

If fresh tomatoes are not available, use 3 quarts of home-canned tomatoes and omit cooking for 25 minutes. For smoother ketchup, use 5 pints of a good quality, no-salt-added canned tomato juice and omit cooking for 25 minutes.

TOMATO KETCHUP

- **1 pouch Mrs. Wages® Ketchup Mix**

- **1½ cups granulated sugar**

- **Approximately 6 pounds fresh, fully ripe tomatoes**

- **1 can (6-ounce) tomato paste**

- **1 cup Mrs. Wages® Pickling & Canning Vinegar or other commercial vinegar (5% acidity)**

1. Combine Mrs. Wages® Ketchup Mix and sugar in a small bowl. Mix well. Set aside.

2. Wash tomatoes carefully. Quarter tomatoes and remove cores. Place in a large saucepan, crushing one layer at a time with a potato masher. Bring crushed tomatoes to boil, stirring frequently. Boil gently for 25 minutes.

3. Press tomatoes through a food mill to separate skins and seeds from juice and pulp. Measure 5 pints (10 cups) juice into 5-quart saucepan. Stir in tomato paste and vinegar. Boil for 20 minutes, stirring frequently. Remove from heat. Slowly add sugar/ketchup seasoning mixture to hot juice, stirring constantly until dry ingredients are uniformly dispersed. Return to heat and boil gently for 5 minutes. Crush any small starch clumps with a spoon against the side of saucepan.

4. To freeze, pour into freezer containers and let cool. Store covered in freezer up to 1 year. Pour boiling hot ketchup into clean, hot pint or half-pint canning jars, leaving ½-inch headspace. Wipe rim clean and adjust lids. Process for 40 minutes in boiling water bath. Boiling water should cover jars by 1-inch. Covered canner should be left on high heat during processing.

5. Test jars for airtight seal 12 to 24 hours after processing. If jars are not properly sealed, refrigerate and use within a week. Label and store in a cool, dry, dark place. Ketchup is ready to eat after 24 hours.

Yield: 5 pints

CHILI SAUCE

- 8 cups chopped ripe tomatoes
- ½ cup chopped sweet red pepper
- ½ cup chopped green bell pepper
- ½ cup chopped onion
- ½ cup granulated sugar
- 1 cup firmly packed brown sugar
- 2 cups cider vinegar (5% acidity)
- 2 teaspoons ground mustard
- 1 teaspoon ground nutmeg
- 1 teaspoon ground cinnamon
- ½ teaspoon cayenne pepper

1. Combine tomatoes, peppers, onion, sugar, brown sugar, vinegar, mustard, nutmeg, cinnamon, and cayenne in a saucepan. Mix thoroughly. Simmer 1 to 2 hours or until mixture reaches desired thickness.

2. Pack the hot sauce into clean, hot canning jars, leaving ½-inch headspace. Wipe rim clean and adjust lids.

3. Process half-pints or pints in a boiling water bath for 15 minutes.

4. Test jars for airtight seal 12 to 24 hours after processing. If jars are not properly sealed, refrigerate and use within a week. Label and store in a cool, dry, dark place.

Yield: 3 pints

NOTES

mrs.wages®

Home Canning

GUIDE AND RECIPES

FRUITS

CANNING FRUITS

There are many different directions for canning fruits with syrup. Here we have given you three options for making syrup: light, medium, and heavy syrup. Please note that fruit may be canned in water – the sugar does not help preserve the fruit, however, sugar does help keep the fruit firm during the canning process.

SYRUP FOR CANNING FRUITS

Heat water to boiling. Dissolve sugar in hot water and cool. Dissolve 1 teaspoon Mrs. Wages® Fresh Fruit Preserver in 1 cup syrup. Prepare and pack fruit according to recipe.

Light Syrup (Best for: Apples, Pears, Grapes)

- 1 cup granulated sugar per quart water

Yield: 4¾ cups syrup

Medium Syrup (Best for: Apricots, Cherries, Grapefruit, Prunes)

- 1³/₄ cups granulated sugar per quart water

Yield: 5¼ cups syrup

Heavy Syrup (Best for: Berries, Figs, Peaches, Plums)

- 2³/₄ cups granulated sugar per quart water

Yield: 5⅓ cups syrup

ASCORBIC ACID MIXTURE FOR PREVENTING DARKENING OF FRUITS

When canning or freezing light-fleshed fruits, often it is recommended to hold the prepared fruit in an ascorbic acid solution to prevent darkening. To make this solution, dissolve 3 tablespoons of Mrs. Wages® Fresh Fruit Preserver in ½ gallon water. Place prepared fruit in this solution.

Apples

1. Wash apples, trim away any bad spots. Peel, core, and cut the fruit into slices, halves, or quarters. Keep prepared fruit in a solution of Mrs. Wages® Fresh Fruit Preserver to prevent discoloration. Drain fruit from solution, and then simmer in a light syrup or water for 4 to 6 minutes. Pack into hot jars while hot. Add boiling syrup, leaving ½-inch headspace. (Use light or medium syrup.)

2. Remove air bubbles. Wipe rims. Adjust lids. Process immediately using boiling water bath method.

Pints... 20 minutes

Quarts..................................... 20 minutes

Applesauce

Use a tart apple variety or a blend of dessert and cooking apples. For each quart of applesauce you will need 2½-3½ pounds of apples. Wash the apples thoroughly, trim away any damaged spots, then quarter and core them. By leaving on the skin, both the flavor and the color of the applesauce will be improved. While cutting apples up, hold those cut in a solution of Mrs. Wages® Fresh Fruit Preserver and water made according to package directions, to prevent darkening. When ready to cook, drain off anti-darkening solution, and place apples in a saucepan. Add 1-inch of water to prevent burning. Simmer until tender, stirring occasionally. Put the apples through a food mill or press. Add sugar and cinnamon to taste. Reheat the sauce just to the boiling point stirring constantly. Ladle hot applesauce into hot jars. Leave ½-inch headspace. Remove air bubbles. Wipe rims. Adjust lids. Process immediately, using boiling water bath method.

Pints... 15 minutes

Quarts..................................... 20 minutes

Apricots

Wash the fruit and remove skins. (Dip them into boiling water for 1 minute then quickly into cold water which permits easy removal of skins.) Cut into halves and remove pits. Slice or leave as halves as desired. Place the peeled fruit into a solution of Mrs. Wages® Fresh Fruit Preserver to prevent discoloration. Drain off anti-darkening solution. Pack raw halves or slices into jars. Cover the fruit with a medium to heavy boiling syrup. Leave ½-inch headspace. Remove air bubbles. Wipe rims. Adjust lids. Process immediately using boiling water bath method.

Pints.. 25 minutes

Quarts....................................... 30 minutes

Berries

Discard all berries that are not completely ripe, are damaged or moldy. Wash berries thoroughly in at least two changes of cold water. Drain. Place the berries in jars. Shake jars to ensure a good fill. Cover berries with boiling light to medium syrup. Leave ½-inch headspace. Remove air bubbles. Wipe rims. Adjust lids. Process immediately using boiling water bath method.

Pints.. 15 minutes

Quarts....................................... 20 minutes

Cherries

Wash fruit, and discard unripe, damaged, or diseased cherries. Remove pits and fill jars leaving ½-inch headspace. Shake jars vigorously to ensure a good fill. Cover cherries with boiling syrup made by dissolving 2½ parts of sugar in 4 parts of water or fruit juice. Leave ½-inch headspace. Remove air bubbles. Wipe rims. Adjust lids. Process immediately using boiling water bath method.

Pints.. 25 minutes

Quarts....................................... 25 minutes

Cranberries

Discard discolored, bruised, or decayed fruit. Wash cranberries thoroughly. Remove all stems and other foreign material. Boil cranberries for 3 minutes in a syrup made by dissolving 1 part of sugar in 1 part of water. Ladle the cooked hot cranberries and syrup into prepared jars. Leave ½-inch headspace. Remove air bubbles. Wipe rims. Adjust lids. Process immediately, using boiling water bath method.

Pints.. 15 minutes

Quarts....................................... 15 minutes

Currants

Wash the currants thoroughly. Discard any off-colored fruit, twigs, or leaves. Remove all stems. Pack currants into prepared jars and cover with a hot medium syrup. Leave ½-inch headspace. Remove air bubbles. Wipe rims. Adjust lids. Process immediately using boiling water bath method.

Pints.. 15 minutes

Quarts.................................... 20 minutes

Figs

Harvest fruit when fully ripe. Remove any damaged, decayed, or green fruit. Cover figs with water and boil 2 minutes. Drain. Gently boil figs in light syrup for 5 minutes. Add ½ teaspoon Mrs. Wages® Citric Acid to each quart jar or ¼ teaspoon per pint jar OR 2 tablespoons lemon juice to each hot quart jar or 1 tablespoon per hot pint jar. Pack hot figs into hot jars leaving ½-inch headspace. Fill jars with hot syrup to within ½-inch from the top. Remove air bubbles. Wipe rims. Adjust lids. Process immediately using boiling water bath method.

Pints.. 45 minutes

Quarts.................................... 50 minutes

Fruit Purées

Use unblemished, ripe fruit. Wash fruit thoroughly, and remove pits or seeds. Cut large fruit into pieces. Simmer until soft, adding a little water at first to keep fruit from sticking and burning. Put cooked fruit through a strainer or food mill. Add sugar to taste. Reheat to simmer. Pour hot purée into hot jars, leaving ½-inch headspace. Remove air bubbles. Wipe rims. Adjust lids. Process immediately using boiling water bath method.

Note:

Fruits not recommended for purée: figs, tomatoes, melon, papaya, mango, coconut or citrus fruits.

Pints.. 15 minutes

Quarts.................................... 15 minutes

Gooseberries

Remove stems and bottom ends of berries, discarding all small, hard, or overripe fruit. Wash fruit. Pack gooseberries into the jars, shaking the jars to ensure a good fill. Cover fruit with boiling medium to heavy syrup. Leave ½-inch headspace. Remove air bubbles. Wipe rims. Adjust lids. Process immediately using boiling water bath method.

Pints.. 15 minutes

Quarts..................................... 20 minutes

Grapes

Stem and wash grapes thoroughly, removing green, decayed, or damaged grapes. Pack into prepared jars. Cover grapes in jars with hot medium syrup. Be sure the syrup is near the boiling point when poured into the hot jars. Leave ½-inch headspace. Remove air bubbles. Wipe rims. Adjust lids. Process immediately using boiling water bath method.

Pints.. 15 minutes

Quarts..................................... 20 minutes

Peaches

Wash fruit. Remove skins. (Put peaches in boiling water for 1 minute. Immediately dip them into cold water for easy removal of the skin.) Trim off discolored or damaged areas. Cut into halves, removing pits. Scrape cavities to remove red fibers. Slice if desired. Place peaches in solution containing Mrs. Wages® Fresh Fruit Preserver to prevent darkening. When ready to can, drain anti-darkening solution, then pack the fruit into prepared jars leaving ½-inch headspace. If packing halves, put them in cut side down. Cover with light to medium boiling syrup. Leave ½-inch headspace. Wipe rims. Remove air bubbles. Adjust lids. Process immediately using boiling water bath method.

Pints.. 25 minutes

Quarts..................................... 30 minutes

Pears

Hot pack is recommended. Make light syrup. Wash, peel, core, and cut pears into halves, quarters, or slices as desired. Put cut pieces into solution containing Mrs. Wages® Fresh Fruit Preserver to prevent discoloration. Drain well. Place the pears in a saucepan and cover with syrup or water. Boil for 5 minutes. Pack pears into hot jars as tightly as possible. Pour boiling hot syrup into the jars, leaving ½-inch headspace. Remove air bubbles. Wipe rims. Adjust lids. Process immediately using boiling water bath method.

Pints.. 20 minutes

Quarts...................................... 25 minutes

Plums

Wash fruit thoroughly, discarding green or decayed fruit. Cut freestone varieties in half and remove pits. Pierce holes in the skins of fruit to be canned whole, to prevent bursting. Pack plums tightly into prepared jars leaving ½-inch headspace. Cover with boiling medium syrup. Leave ½-inch headspace. Remove air bubbles. Wipe rims. Adjust lids. Process immediately, using the boiling water bath method.

Pints.. 20 minutes

Quarts...................................... 25 minutes

Rhubarb

Wash rhubarb stalks thoroughly, discarding any damaged stalks. Cut into ½-inch pieces. In a large bowl, combine ½ cup granulated sugar with each quart of rhubarb, cover and let stand in refrigerator for several hours to draw out the juice. Pour rhubarb and sugar into a saucepan and bring to boil. Pack hot rhubarb tightly into prepared hot jars, leaving ½-inch headspace. Remove air bubbles. Wipe rims. Adjust lids. Process immediately using boiling water bath method.

Pints.. 15 minutes

Quarts...................................... 15 minutes

Strawberries

Canning strawberries is not recommended. Instead, freeze them or make them into jams or jellies.

Note:

Suggested apples: Fuji, McIntosh, Jonagold, Rome, Cameo, Jonathon, Red Delicious, Honeycrisp or Pink Ladies. Use a mixture of varieties for best flavor.

Note:

Peaches or pears may also be used for pie fillings.

MRS. WAGES® APPLE PIE FILLING

- **4-5 pounds of apples**
- **3 cups granulated sugar**
- **3 cups water or apple juice**
- **1 pouch Mrs. Wages® Fruit Pie Filling Mix**

1. Peel, core, and slice 4 to 5 pounds apples to yield about 3 pounds apple slices. Blanch apple slices in hot water (200°F) for 1 minute. Drain, reserving juice, and keep in covered pan.

2. In a large saucepan, whisk together sugar, water or reserved apple juice, and Mrs. Wages® Fruit Pie Filling Mix. Cook over medium heat (180°F) stirring constantly until thickened. Remove from heat. Add apple slices and stir to coat.

3. Ladle apple mixture into hot jars leaving 1-inch headspace. Remove air bubbles, wipe rims, add lid and ring. Process pints or quarts for 25 minutes in boiling water bath. Cool overnight and test for seals.

4. Use product for pies, tarts, cake, crisps, cobblers and other desserts.

Yield: 3 quarts

MRS. WAGES® SPICED APPLESAUCE

- **8-10 pounds apples**
- **2 cups water**
- **granulated sugar**
- **1 pouch Mrs. Wages® Spiced Apple Mix**

Note:
Suggested apple varieties: Red Delicious, Gala, Fuji, Winesap, McIntosh, Yellow Delicious, Mutsu, Pink Lady and Honeycrisp.

1. Wash, core, and peel apples. Cut into halves or quarters. Combine prepared apples and water in a large saucepan. Bring to boil. Cover, reduce heat and simmer for 30 minutes or until apples are soft. Purée apple mixture and measure number of cups before returning to pan. Add ¼ cup sugar per 1 cup purée. Stir to dissolve sugar. Stir in Mrs. Wages® Spiced Apple Mix and heat just to a boil. Remove from heat.

2. Ladle hot mixture into prepared hot jars, leaving ½-inch headspace. Remove air bubbles, wipe rims, and adjust lids and rings. Process pints for 15 minutes and quarts for 20 minutes in boiling water bath canner. Cool overnight. Test for airtight seal after 24 hours. If jars have not sealed, refrigerate and use within 2 weeks.

Yield: 3 quarts

SPICED APPLE OR PEAR BUTTER

- 8-10 pounds Fuji, Red/Yellow Delicious, or Gala apples or Bartlett pears
- 2 cups apple cider vinegar
- 2 cups water
- 5 cups granulated sugar
- 1 pouch Mrs. Wages® Spiced Apple Mix

1. Wash and quarter apples or pears. Do not peel or core because the pectin in the peel is needed in this recipe.

2. Combine prepared apples or pears, apple cider vinegar, and water in a large, wide-bottomed pan. Bring to boil. Cover, reduce heat and simmer for 30 to 40 minutes until apples or pears are soft. Stir mixture occasionally for even cooking.

3. Transfer fruit mixture to food mill and purée to separate seeds and peels. A colander or strainer may also be used to press the mixture through. Discard seeds and peels.

4. Measure 5 quarts of puréed fruit mixture (20 cups) and return to saucepan. Stir in sugar and Mrs. Wages® Spiced Apple Mix until well combined. Cook mixture, uncovered, over medium heat, stirring frequently to prevent burning. Cook about 3 to 4 hours until mixture is thickened and smooth, and much of the moisture has evaporated.

5. Ladle hot mixture into prepared hot jars, leaving ¼-inch headspace. Remove air bubbles, wipe rims, and adjust lids and rings. Process half-pints and pints for 15 minutes and quarts for 20 minutes in boiling water bath canner. Cool overnight. Test for airtight seal after 24 hours. If jars have not sealed, refrigerate and use within 2 weeks.

Yield: 3 quarts

MRS. WAGES® FOREST BERRY PIE FILLING

- 3½-4 pounds berries or cherries

- 3 cups granulated sugar

- 3 cups water or bottled fruit juice

- 1 pouch Mrs. Wages® Forest Berry Pie Filling Mix

1. Wash berries or cherries. Pit cherries and blanch in hot water (200°F) for 1 minute, drain and keep in covered pot. Do not blanch blueberries, raspberries and blackberries. Do not use strawberries.

2. Combine sugar and Mrs. Wages® Forest Berry Pie Filling Mix in a large non-reactive saucepan. Do not use aluminum. Whisk dry mixture together. Stir in water or fruit juice. Cook mixture over medium heat (180°F), stirring constantly, until thickened. Tip: DO NOT overcook the mixture. Remove from heat. Fold prepared berries or cherries into hot sauce mixture.

3. Ladle hot mixture carefully into hot jars, filling evenly. Leave 1-inch headspace. Remove air bubbles, wipe rim and cap each jar as it is filled.

4. Process pints or quarts 30 minutes in a boiling water bath canner. Turn off heat, carefully remove canner lid and let jars stand for 5 minutes in canner. Remove jars. Let jars sit undisturbed to cool at room temperature for 12 to 24 hours. Test jars for airtight seals according to manufacturer's directions. If jars do not completely seal, refrigerate and consume within 2 weeks.

5. Product is ready to eat after 24 hours. Store properly processed shelf-stable product in a cool place, and use within 1 year. Prepared pie filling can be used for pies, tarts, crisps, cobblers and other desserts.

Yield: 3 quarts

MRS. WAGES® SPICED PEACHES

- 10-12 pounds peaches (about 25 medium)
- 2½ cups granulated sugar
- 4½ cups water
- ⅔ cup Mrs. Wages® Pickling & Canning Vinegar or other commercial white vinegar (5% acidity)
- 1 pouch Mrs. Wages® Spiced Peaches Mix

1. Wash peaches, peel, remove pit and cut into six slices. This should yield at least 16 cups peach slices.

2. Combine sugar, water, vinegar and Mrs. Wages® Spiced Peaches Mix in a large non-reactive saucepan. Do not use aluminum. Bring mixture just to a boil over medium heat, stirring often. Add prepared peaches and return to boil. Reduce heat and simmer (200°F) for 5 minutes. Remove from heat.

3. Ladle hot peach slices carefully into hot jars, filling evenly. If more liquid is needed for proper headspace, add a mixture of 1 part hot vinegar and 7 parts hot water. Leave ½-inch headspace. Remove air bubbles, wipe rim and cap each jar as it is filled.

4. Process pints 20 minutes, quarts 25 minutes in a boiling water bath canner. Turn off heat, carefully remove canner lid and let jars stand for 5 minutes in canner. Remove jars. Let jars sit undisturbed to cool at room temperature for 12 to 24 hours. Test jars for airtight seals according to manufacturer's directions. If jars do not completely seal, refrigerate and consume within 2 weeks.

5. Product is ready to eat after 24 hours. Store properly processed shelf-stable product in a cool place, and use within 1 year.

Yield: 6 quarts

SECTION 3

mrs.wages®

Home Canning
GUIDE AND RECIPES

VEGETABLES

CANNING VEGETABLES

Since all vegetables except tomatoes are low-acid foods, they must be processed in a pressure canner. The higher temperatures achieved in a pressure canner are necessary to destroy the c. botulinum spores that may be present in these foods.

As stated before, it is imperative that you follow canning directions exactly. Adding extra vegetables, meats, or other foods to home-canned goods before processing, may mean serious illness or even death to the individuals who consume them. While many individuals may have used other canning methods in the past with no bad results, it will take only one jar of food containing deadly bacteria to cause illness.

Each year, before the canning season begins, take out your pressure canner and examine it carefully. If the gaskets seem a little stiff or are cracked, replace them. If you have a dial gauge canner, check with your local Extension office or stores that sell canners to see if they have a way to test your canner for accuracy.

As with all foods you are preserving for future use, foods for canning should be at peak quality. Food does not improve with canning so starting with moldy or damaged vegetables is not a good idea. Follow the directions carefully and you should have good results—food that is wholesome without extra additives and preservatives.

When you are ready to eat your home-canned food, if the jar is leaking, unsealed, bubbling, frothy, or has an off-odor, do not taste it—throw it away! As with all things, if in doubt, throw it out.

Step by step instructions for using the pressure canner can be found on pages 21-23 in this canning guide.

ASPARAGUS

1. Wash asparagus, remove scales and tough ends. Asparagus may be canned either as whole spears or cut into 1-inch pieces. Use tender spears, 4 to 6 inches in length.

2. Hot pack: place asparagus in pan and cover with boiling water. Boil 2 to 3 minutes. Loosely fill prepared jars with hot asparagus leaving 1-inch headspace.

3. Raw Pack: place prepared asparagus into hot jars, filling as tightly as possible but do not crush. Leave 1-inch headspace.

4. If desired, add Mrs. Wages® Pickling & Canning Salt; up to ½ teaspoon per pint or 1 teaspoon per quart. Add boiling water leaving 1-inch of headspace. Remove any air bubbles and adjust headspace if needed. Wipe rims with dry paper towel. Adjust lids and process in a pressure canner (dial or weighted gauge).

Pints................ 30 minutes at 240°F. (10 pounds PSI)

Quarts............. 40 minutes at 240°F. (10 pounds PSI)

BEANS

• Snap, green or wax beans

1. Snap beans make the most tender canned product. Use only those beans that break easily when bent double. Wash beans, trim off ends, then cut pods to desired length.

2. *Hot Pack:* Place the beans in a saucepan and cover with boiling water; boil for 5 minutes. Pack into hot jars leaving 1-inch headspace.

3. *Raw Pack:* Tightly fill hot jars with raw beans; leave 1-inch headspace.

4. If desired, add Mrs. Wages® Pickling & Canning Salt; up to ½ teaspoon per pint or 1 teaspoon per quart. Add boiling water, leaving 1-inch headspace. Remove air bubbles and wipe rims with damp paper towel. Adjust lids and process in pressure canner (dial or weighted gauge).

Pints................ 20 minutes at 240°F. (10 pounds PSI)

Quarts............. 25 minutes at 240°F. (10 pounds PSI)

BEANS

- **Fresh shelled lima beans**

1. Wash beans, then shell, discarding any bad beans. Wash again.

2. Hot Pack: Place beans in saucepan and cover with boiling water and heat to a boil. Drain and place hot beans loosely into hot jars. Leave 1-inch headspace.

3. Raw Pack: Fill hot jars with raw beans—do not shake down or press.

4. Small beans-leave 1-inch of headspace for pints and 1½-inch for quarts

5. Large beans-leave 1-inch headspace for pints and 1¼-inch for quarts

6. If desired, add Mrs. Wages® Pickling & Canning Salt; up to ½ teaspoon per pint or 1 teaspoon per quart. Add boiling water leaving headspace as described above. Remove air bubbles and wipe rims with damp paper towel, adjust lids and process in pressure canner (either dial or weighted gauge).

Pints................ 40 minutes at 240°F. (10 pounds PSI)

Quarts............. 50 minutes at 240°F. (10 pounds PSI)

DRIED BEANS

- **Kidney beans, lima beans, navy beans, southern peas, and Great Northern beans**

1. Wash and sort dried beans, discarding discolored beans and stones. Place beans or peas in a large saucepan and cover with water. Soak for 12 to 18 hours in a cool place (refrigerator is great). Drain off soaking water and cover beans with fresh water. Bring to boil. Boil for 2 minutes. Remove from heat and let soak for 1 hour; drain. Cover beans with fresh water and boil 30 minutes.

2. If desired, add Mrs. Wages® Pickling & Canning Salt; ½ teaspoon per pint or 1 teaspoon per quart to the hot jars. Fill hot jars with beans or peas and cooking water, leaving 1-inch headspace. Remove air bubbles and wipe rims with a damp paper towel. Adjust lids and process in pressure canner (either dial or weighted gauge).

Pints................ 75 minutes at 240°F. (10 pounds PSI)

Quarts............. 90 minutes at 240°F. (10 pounds PSI)

BEETS

- **Small, tender beets**

1. Small, tender beets have the best quality after canning. Cut the tops off, leaving 1 inch of stem and the roots. Wash beets then place them in a saucepan of boiling water. Boil until the skins slip off, about 15 to 25 minutes.

2. Remove skins, stems and rootend. Small and medium sizes may be canned whole. Large beets should be quartered, cubed, or sliced. Add Mrs. Wages® Pickling & Canning Salt to the hot jars; ½ teaspoon per pint or 1 teaspoon per quart. Pack hot beets into prepared jars and add fresh hot water, leaving 1-inch of headspace. Remove air bubbles and wipe rims with a damp paper towel. Adjust lids and process in a pressure canner (dial or weighted gauge).

   Pints............... 30 minutes at 240°F. (10 pounds PSI)
   Quarts............. 35 minutes at 240°F. (10 pounds PSI)

CARROTS

- **Small carrots, 1 to 1 ¼-inches in diameter**

1. Wash, peel and then rewash the carrots. Slice or dice.

2. Hot Pack: Place carrots in saucepan and cover with boiling water; bring to boil and simmer for 5 minutes. Fill hot jars leaving 1-inch headspace.

3. Raw Pack: Fill hot jars tightly with raw carrots; leave 1-inch headspace.

4. If desired, add Mrs. Wages® Pickling & Canning Salt; ½ teaspoon per pint or 1 teaspoon per quart to the hot jars. Cover with boiling water; leaving 1-inch headspace. Remove air bubbles and wipe rims with damp paper towel. Adjust lids and process in a pressure canner (dial or weighted gauge).

   Pints............... 25 minutes at 240°F. (10 pounds PSI)
   Quarts............. 30 minutes at 240°F. (10 pounds PSI)

CORN — CREAM STYLE CORN

- **Fresh corn**

1. Only can in pint jars. The length of time it would take to can quarts destroys flavor and food value.

2. Select corn that is slightly immature or at its prime for eating. Husk and remove silk. Wash. Cut off top halves of the kernels; scrape off the rest of the corn with the back of a knife. Measure corn and scrapings.

3. Place corn and scrapings into a saucepan, adding 1 cup of boiling water to each 2 cups of corn. Stirring constantly, bring mixture to boil. Add up to 1 teaspoon Mrs. Wages® Pickling & Canning Salt and 2 teaspoons of sugar to each hot pint jar if desired. Fill pint jars with hot corn mixture, leaving 1-inch headspace. Remove air bubbles and wipe rims with damp paper towel. Adjust lids and process in a pressure canner (dial or weighted gauge).

   Pints............... 85 minutes at 240°F. (10 pounds PSI)

Note:

Sweeter varieties of corn or immature corn may result in browning of the canned product. Make a small test batch of these to check the product before doing larger quantities.

CORN — WHOLE KERNEL CORN

- **Fresh corn**

1. Husk corn and remove silk. Wash. Blanch ears for 3 minutes in boiling water. Cut kernels from cob about ¾ the depth of the kernel. Do not scrape cob.

2. Hot pack: To each quart of kernels in saucepan, add 1 cup hot water and heat to boiling. Simmer for 5 minutes. Fill hot jars with hot corn and cooking liquid, leaving 1-inch of headspace.

3. Raw Pack: Fill hot jars with raw kernels leaving 1-inch of headspace. Do not shake or press down.

4. If desired, add Mrs. Wages® Pickling & Canning Salt to the hot jars; ½ teaspoon per pint or 1 teaspoon per quart. Add fresh boiling water, leaving 1-inch of headspace. Remove air bubbles and wipe rims with a damp paper towel. Adjust lids and process in a pressure canner (dial or weighted gauge).

   Pints............... 55 minutes at 240°F. (10 pounds PSI)
   Quarts............ 85 minutes at 240°F. (10 pounds PSI)

GREENS

- Mustard, turnips, dandelion, beet tops, spinach, kale, collards, Swiss chard, and other leafy green produce

1. Use freshly picked, green leaves. Remove tough stems and discolored leaves. Wash thoroughly through several changes of water. Place greens in a cheesecloth bag and steam them in a large stockpot for 10 minutes or until they are well wilted. Pack greens loosely in hot jars. Cover with boiling water, leaving 1-inch headspace. If desired, add Mrs. Wages® Pickling & Canning Salt, ½ teaspoon per pint or 1 teaspoon per quart. Remove air bubbles and wipe rims with a damp paper towel. Adjust lids and process in a pressure canner (dial or gauge type).

Pints............... 70 minutes at 240°F. (10 pounds PSI)

Quarts............ 90 minutes at 240°F. (10 pounds PSI)

MUSHROOMS

- Small to medium size domestic mushrooms

Note:
Do not can wild mushrooms.

1. Select brightly-colored, small to medium sized domestic mushrooms with short stems, closed caps, and showing no signs of discoloration. Soak mushrooms in cold water for 10 minutes to remove soil. Wash in clean water. Leave small mushrooms whole and cut larger ones in halves or quarters. Cover with water in a saucepan and boil for 5 minutes.

2. Fill prepared jars with hot mushrooms. Add ½ teaspoon Mrs. Wages® Pickling & Canning Salt to each pint, if desired. For better color, add 1 teaspoon Mrs. Wages® Fresh Fruit Preserver (ascorbic acid) to each jar. Add boiling hot cooking liquid or fresh boiling water to cover mushrooms leaving 1-inch headspace. Remove air bubbles and wipe rims with damp paper towel. Adjust lids and process in a pressure canner (dial or weighted gauge).

Pints/half pints....45 minutes at 240°F. (10 pounds PSI)

OKRA

- **Okra**

1. Can okra as quickly as possible after picking. Can only tender pods. Trim stems. Use only stainless steel knives. Iron, even water that is high in iron, will cause discoloration.

2. Wash pods and trim stems. Leave whole or cut into 1-inch pieces. Cover with hot water in a saucepan and boil for 2 minutes. Drain, reserving liquid. Fill hot jars with hot okra and cooking liquid, leaving 1-inch headspace. Add Mrs. Wages® Pickling & Canning Salt, ½ teaspoon per pint or 1 teaspoon per quart if desired. Remove air bubbles and wipe rims with damp paper towel. Adjust lids and process in a pressure canner (dial or weighted gauge).

   Pints or Quarts.................40 minutes at 240°F. (10 pounds PSI)

PEAS

- **Southern peas, black-eyed peas, cow peas, and crowder peas**

1. Shell and wash peas discarding any damaged peas.

2. Hot Pack: Place peas in saucepan and cover with boiling water. Bring to a boil and boil for 2 minutes. Fill hot jars loosely with hot peas and add cooking liquid, leaving 1-inch headspace.

3. Raw Pack: Fill hot jars with raw peas and add boiling water, leaving 1-inch headspace. Do not shake or compact peas.

4. If desired, add Mrs. Wages® Pickling & Canning Salt to hot jars, ½ teaspoon per pint or 1 teaspoon per quart. Process in a pressure canner (dial or weighted gauge).

   Pints or Quarts.................40 minutes at 240°F. (10 pounds PSI)

PEPPERS

- **Bell, yellow, sweet red, orange, or purple peppers**

1. Wash and drain sweet bell peppers. Remove stems and seeds. Cut into desired size. Blanch for 3 minutes in boiling water, drain.

2. Pack peppers loosely into hot jars, leaving 1-inch headspace. Add Mrs. Wages® Pickling & Canning Salt, ½ teaspoon per pint, if desired. Add cooking liquid or boiling water, leaving 1-inch headspace. Remove air bubbles and wipe rims with damp paper towels. Adjust lids and process in pressure canner (dial or weighted gauge).

   Pints............... 35 minutes at 240°F. (10 pounds PSI)

POTATOES

- **White or Irish potatoes**

Note: Potatoes that have been stored at 45°F or below may discolor when canned.

1. Select small to medium-sized potatoes. Wash and peel potatoes. Small potatoes, 1 to 2 inches in diameter may be canned whole. Cut larger potatoes into 1-inch cubes.

2. Hot Pack: Place prepared potatoes in a solution of 1 teaspoon Mrs. Wages® Fresh Fruit Preserver dissolved in 1 gallon of water to help prevent darkening. Drain. Place potatoes in saucepan of hot water and bring to a boil. Boil whole potatoes for 10 minutes and cubes for 2 minutes. Drain. Pack hot potatoes into hot jars, leaving 1-inch headspace.

3. If desired, add Mrs. Wages® Pickling & Canning Salt, ½ teaspoon per pint or 1 teaspoon per quart. Add fresh boiling water leaving 1-inch headspace. Remove bubbles and wipe rims with damp paper towel. Adjust lids and process in a pressure canner (dial or gauge).

   Pints............... 35 minutes at 240°F. (10 pounds PSI)
   Quarts............ 40 minutes at 240°F. (10 pounds PSI)

PUMPKIN AND WINTER SQUASH

1. Wash, remove seeds, and cut into 1-inch slices and pare. Cut flesh into 1-inch cubes. Place in a saucepan and cover with water. Boil for 2 minutes. Drain, reserving liquid. Do not mash or purée.

2. Pack hot cubes into hot jars. Add Mrs. Wages® Pickling & Canning Salt, ½ teaspoon per pint or 1 teaspoon per quart, if desired. Cover with reserved hot cooking liquid or fresh boiling water, leaving 1-inch headspace. Remove air bubbles and wipe rims with damp paper towel. Adjust lids and process in a pressure canner (dial or gauge type).

   Pints................ 55 minutes at 240°F. (10 pounds PSI)
   Quarts............. 90 minutes at 240°F. (10 pounds PSI)

SWEET POTATOES

1. Sweet potatoes should be canned within 2 months of harvest. Select small to medium sweet potatoes.

2. Wash potatoes and boil or steam until partially soft about 15 to 20 minutes. Cool until safely handled. Peel, remove any damaged parts, and cut into desired size. Dip in a solution of Mrs. Wages® Fresh Fruit Preserver made of 1 teaspoon preserver to 1 pint of water to prevent darkening.

3. Do not purée potatoes.

4. Fill hot jars with hot potato pieces, leaving 1-inch headspace. Add Mrs. Wages® Pickling & Canning Salt, ½ teaspoon per pint or 1 teaspoon per quart, if desired. Fill jars with hot boiling water OR boiling syrup made of 1 part sugar to 2 parts water, leaving 1-inch headspace. Remove air bubbles and wipe rim with damp paper towel. Adjust lids and process in a pressure canner (dial or gauge type).

   Pints................ 65 minutes at 240°F. (10 pounds PSI)
   Quarts............. 90 minutes at 240°F. (10 pounds PSI)

Home Canning

GUIDE AND RECIPES

CHICKEN, MEAT AND SEAFOOD

CANNING MEAT AND POULTRY

No cookbook on canning would be complete without some mention of canning meat and poultry.

All poultry, meat, game, and seafood are low-acid foods and must be processed in a pressure canner. If you have never tasted home canned meat before, you may be in for a surprise. Home canned meats are extremely tender and tasty. In the past, meat canned at home was a staple for many meals because it was ready to heat and eat. Today, while the process may be a little long, home-processed meats are becoming more popular as a preservation method.

As with any food for preserving, start with the best quality you can afford. Keep meats refrigerated at 40°F or below prior to the canning process to preserve freshness. Start with a clean (sanitized) kitchen and keep all food, surfaces, and utensils clean to prevent bacterial contamination.

If you need to wait a few days before canning meat, freeze it to maintain freshness. When you are ready to begin canning meat, trim off all visible fat and any bruises or tough gristly spots. The fat that is left in the meat can go up the sides of the jar; fat that comes into contact with the lid may cause seal failure.

For more information on canning meats, poultry and wild game at home, contact your local Cooperative Extension Service office.

CHICKEN
(USDA COMPLETE GUIDE TO HOME CANNING)

1. Chicken to be canned should be as fresh as possible. Freshly killed and dressed chicken should be chilled for 6 to 12 hours before the canning process. Purchased fresh chicken may also be canned. Remove any visible fat. Cut the meat into sizes that are suitable for canning. Can with or without bone.

2. Hot Pack: Boil, steam, or bake the chicken until it is about two-thirds done. Fill prepared jars with hot meat and broth, leaving 1¼-inch headspace. Add Mrs. Wages® Pickling & Canning Salt; ½ teaspoon per pint or 1 teaspoon per quart, if desired. Fill jars to within 1¼-inches of the top with hot broth. Remove any air bubbles and wipe jar rims with damp paper towel; adjust lids.

3. Raw Pack: Add Mrs. Wages® Pickling & Canning Salt; ½ teaspoon per pint or 1 teaspoon per quart to the hot jars if desired. Loosely fill hot jars with raw meat, leaving 1¼-inch headspace. Do not add liquid. Wipe jar rims with damp paper towel and adjust lids.

4. Process in a pressure canner at 11 pounds for dial type canners and 10 pounds for weighted gauge canners.

Without Bones
Pints..75 minutes
Quarts...90 minutes

With Bones
Pints..65 minutes
Quarts...75 minutes

GROUND OR CHOPPED MEAT
(USDA COMPLETE GUIDE TO HOME CANNING)

1. You will have better quality meat if you freeze ground or chopped meats. For canning, choose fresh, chilled meat. If you are canning venison, one part high-quality pork fat to three or four parts venison should be added prior to grinding.

2. Hot Pack: Shape meat into patties or balls then cook until lightly brown. Ground meat may be sautéed without shaping. Remove any excess fat.
Fill prepared jars loosely with pieces of hot meat leaving 1-inch headspace. Add boiling meat broth, tomato juice or water leaving 1-inch headspace.
Add Mrs. Wages® Pickling & Canning Salt to jars; ½ teaspoon per pint or 1 teaspoon per quart, if desired. Remove air bubbles and wipe rims with damp paper towel and adjust lids.

3. Process in a dial type pressure canner at 11 pounds or a weighted gauge canner at 10 pounds pressure:

Pints..75 minutes
Quarts...90 minutes

STRIPS OR CUBES OF MEAT
(USDA COMPLETE GUIDE TO HOME CANNING)

Choose quality meats. Remove excess fat. Strong-flavored wild meats should be soaked for 1 hour in brine made from 1 tablespoon of salt per quart of water. Rinse meat. Remove bones.

Hot Pack: Pre-cook meat to the rare stage by roasting, stewing, or browning in a small amount of fat. Add Mrs. Wages® Pickling & Canning Salt to each jar; ½ teaspoon per pint or 1 teaspoon per quart, if desired. Fill prepared jars with pieces and add boiling meat broth, water, or tomato juice, leaving 1-inch headspace. (Note: wild game is best when packed with tomato juice.) Remove air bubbles and wipe rims with a damp paper towel. Adjust lids and process in a pressure canner.

Raw Pack: Add Mrs. Wages® Pickling & Canning Salt to each hot jar; ½ teaspoon per pint or 1 teaspoon per quart, if desired. Fill jars with raw meat pieces leaving 1-inch headspace. Do not add liquid. Wipe rims of jars with damp paper towels. Adjust lids and process in a pressure canner.

Process in a dial gauge canner at 11 pounds pressure or a weighted gauge canner at 10 pounds pressure:

Pints..75 minutes
Quarts ....90 minutes

VEGETABLE SOUPS

Having a favorite vegetable soup ready for reheating can help you get a meal on the table in fairly short order. While many commercial soups are available, some individuals are concerned with the sodium content along with other preservatives added to the food. Homemade vegetable soup is possible if you take a few precautions in the making.

Keep in mind the foods you will be using are low acid and must be processed in a pressure canner. Certain ingredients including thickening agents, milk, cream, flour, rice, noodles and other pasta should NOT be added to the soup before canning. These ingredients may be added just prior to serving the soup.

BEEF-VEGETABLE SOUP

- 1½ pounds very lean roast beef, remove all visible fat and small cubed
- ¾ cup chopped onion
- 1 cup peeled carrot slices
- 1 cup celery slices
- 2 Roma tomatoes, cubed
- 4 cups seasoned tomato-vegetable juice blend (low sodium)
- 2 cups water
- Mrs. Wages® Pickling & Canning Salt (to taste)
- Seasoning to taste (garlic powder, dried oregano, dried basil, pepper, etc.)

1. Prepare each vegetable as for hot pack canning. In a large stockpot, cook meat until brown. Add onions, carrots, celery, tomatoes, tomato juice, water, salt and seasonings. Bring to boil. Boil for 5 minutes.

2. Remove hot jars from water and drain. Fill hot jars half way with solids from soup, then continue filling with hot liquid leaving 1-inch headspace. Remove any air bubbles. Wipe jar rims with clean damp paper towels. Adjust lids and process at 11 pounds pressure in a dial gauge pressure canner or at 10 pounds in a weighted gauge canner.

Pints..60 minutes
Quarts...75 minutes

Yield: 5-6 pints

NOTES

mrs.wages®

Home Canning
GUIDE AND RECIPES

PICKLES
AND RELISHES

PICKLES AND RELISHES

To add zest to your meals, try serving your own homemade pickles. They will enliven mundane meals and brighten salads–and they make delightful gifts. Now, thanks to Mrs. Wages® pickling products, pickles are easy to make, and even beginners don't have to worry about failures, as they follow the simple instructions.

Most of the recipes are for fresh-pack pickles. This means they are made from produce that is packed raw into the jars. Often vegetables are short-brined, covered with salt and allowed to stand for a couple of hours before packing. That makes them crisp. Then, raw or brined, pickles are put into jars, a boiling syrup or brine is poured over top, and the jars are sealed and processed, using the boiling water bath canning method.

Also included are recipes for the traditional brined pickles, the ones you used to find in the big crocks and jars at the general store. Using this method, you cure the vegetables, usually cucumbers, for several weeks in a brine. Then you pack the vegetables into jars and either process them or refrigerate them.

The difference between a good pickle and a great one is usually the freshness of the ingredients. Select young or even slightly immature, undamaged fruits and vegetables. Harvest them early in the day, if you are picking from your home garden and process immediately. If you buy the produce at a farmer's market or supermarket, refrigerate it until you are ready to use it. Scrub it thoroughly with a vegetable brush, then rinse it, preferably under running water, and drain it in a colander. Remove the 1/16-inch from the blossom ends of cucumbers.

Cucumbers
Pickling cucumbers are preferred for making pickles. You can identify slicing cucumbers by their dark green color and are typically 6 to 8 inches in length. Pickling cucumbers are short and blocky. If you are growing cucumbers to make pickles, choose the pickling types. These cucumbers were developed to go through the brining process and will generally produce a higher quality product. If you intend to use your home-grown cucumbers in salads, then select the slicing types. In general, burpless cucumbers are not suitable for making pickles.

Vinegar

Use quality commercially available vinegar that has 5% acetic acid. Mrs. Wages®
Pickling & Canning Vinegar (5% acidity) is best for most pickles, particularly white
pickles such as cauliflower, since it does not discolor them. Cider vinegar (5%) is
recommended for many sweet pickle and chutney recipes, but it will darken the
produce. The more expensive malt vinegar will also darken pickles, but it is often
recommended because of its delicate, sweet flavor.

Herbs and Spices

While many old-fashioned recipes call for combinations of herbs and spices, some
of our pickling recipes are made easier by calling for the use of Mrs. Wages® Quick
Process Pickle Mixes. You have a choice of many varieties of mixes. Each assures
you perfect pickles and consistent flavor with each batch.

Salt

We recommend Mrs. Wages® Pickling & Canning Salt, packaged expressly for
making pickles. Ordinary table salt should not be used because of its iodine and
anti-caking additives that may cause off colors and cloudiness.

Equipment

A food processor, while not essential, will save you a lot of time if the recipe calls
for cutting a quantity of vegetables. A boiling water bath canner is used for most
of the recipes. Standard canning jars with two-piece lids should be used. Crocks of
glass, plastic, or ceramic may be used for slow-brining pickles. Use stainless steel,
glass, or ceramic pans, bowls and utensils. The salts and acids in pickles react
with metals other than stainless steel to produce an off flavor.

Other utensils that you should have are a wide mouth funnel and a wooden spoon
for neat and firm packing of the vegetables, a jar lifter, and a non-metal spatula,
or a plastic bubble freer, to rid the produce of air bubbles in the jar before the lid
is put on.

CANNING PICKLES

STEP BY STEP INSTRUCTIONS:

Follow the steps listed below, making changes only when specifically told to do so in the recipe, and you will have pickles you will be proud to serve.

1. Read the recipe. Familiarize yourself with the process, the equipment you need and the ingredients.

2. Lay out the equipment.

3. Prepare the cucumbers. Scrub them with a vegetable brush, then rinse, and drain in a colander.

4. Remove $\frac{1}{16}$-inch from the blossom end of the cucumber to prevent soft pickles.

5. Cut the cucumbers according to directions in the recipe.

6. If the directions call for it, salt the cucumbers, or chill them in ice water. Never take shortcuts.

7. Wash jars, lids, and screw bands in hot, soapy water, rinse well.

8. Prepare and process home canning jars and lids according to manufacturer's instructions for sterilized jars. Keep jars hot.

9. If recipe calls for sterilized jars, put them in hot water, bring to a boil, and boil for 15 minutes. Keep them in that hot water until ready for use.

10. Fill canner half full of water, bring water to a boil, then keep it hot. Heat another stockpot of water.

11. Make brine or syrup, as called for in the recipe. Cook this, if necessary.

12. Working with only two or three jars at a time, pack the cucumbers firmly in them, leaving the correct amount of headspace.

13. Add brine or syrup as directed in the recipe.

14. Run a plastic bubble freer around the inside of each jar to release any air bubbles.

15. Add more brine or syrup, if needed to maintain the proper headspace.

16. Wipe the top of each jar with a damp paper towel if your syrup contains sugar, or with a dry paper towel if not. Do this thoroughly and carefully to prevent small particles from interfering with the seal.

17. Center the lid over the mouth of each jar. Screw the band down firmly.

18. Lower the jars into the simmering (not boiling) water with a jar lifter. Make sure jars are not touching to get good heat circulation. A wire basket will keep the jars properly spaced.

19. Add hot water if needed to cover jars by one to two inches. Put on the lid, and bring water to a rolling boil.

20. When water is at a full boil, begin timing.

21. When the recommended time is up, remove the canner from the heat, remove the lid and leave the jars in the canner for an additional 5 minutes before removing them from the canner. Use a jar lifter to remove the jars without tilting the jars.

22. Put the jars on a cake rack or towel in a draft-free area. Do not bump them together; they will shatter easily when hot. Do not cover them. Do not turn them upside down.

23. Allow the jars to cool for 12 to 24 hours.

24. Test the seal. The center on the lid of the two-piece screw band jars should be depressed. Remove the screw band.

25. Wash the jars, label them with the date, and variety of pickles. Store in a cool, dark, dry place.

26. Jars with defective seals should be stored in the refrigerator, and contents eaten within two weeks.

LOW-SALT BRINING

Those old-time pickles that came in the big barrel were brined, left to ferment in a salt solution for as many as six weeks, depending on the recipe. And, while cucumbers are the most common vegetable that is brined, others can be as well.

STEP BY STEP INSTRUCTIONS:

Here are the steps for low-salt brining:

1. Wash the vegetables. Remove ⅟₁₆-inch from the blossom end of cucumbers.

2. Weigh the vegetables.

3. Scrub the crock with hot, soapy water, rinse it with hot water, then scald it with boiling water, and dry it.

4. Prepare the brine according to the recipe directions. Using Mrs. Wages® Pickling & Canning Salt. Allow the brine to cool.

5. Layer the vegetables and spices in the crock, following recipe directions. Leave at least 4 inches of space at the top.

6. Pour the cooled brine over the vegetables, making sure it covers them.

7. Hold the vegetables under the brine with a weighted plate. Store in a cool, dark, dry place.

8. Fermentation will begin in about three days. Remove any scum from the top of the brine daily.

9. Fermentation is complete when bubbles stop rising to the top of the crock, usually after two to four weeks.

10. To keep these pickles, process them using the boiling water bath method. Pack the pickles into clean, hot canning jars. Strain the brine and bring it to a boil. Pour it over the pickles, leaving ¼-inch headspace. Remove bubbles and wipe the rim of the jar. Adjust the lid. Process for 15 minutes.

Problem	Diagnosis	Remedy
Soft or slippery pickles Spoilage evident (do not use)	Brine too weak.	Maintain 10-12% salt concentration.
	Vinegar too weak.	Use vinegar of 5% acidity.
	Cucumbers stored at a temperature too high during curing/brining.	About 70-75°F appears to be the best since this is the optimum temperature for growth of the organisms necessary for fermentation.
	Insufficient amount of brine.	Keep cucumbers immersed in the brine.
	Pickles not processed properly (to destroy microorganisms).	See section on processing pickles.
	Failure to remove ¹⁄₁₆-inch from blossom end.	Remove ¹⁄₁₆-inch from blossom end.
Strong, bitter taste	Spices cooked too long in vinegar, or too many spices used.	Follow directions for amount of spices to use and the boiling time.
	Vinegar too strong.	Strong vinegars should be diluted to proper strength (5% acidity).
Hollow pickles	Large sizes will float at 10-12% brine solution.	Use smaller cucumbers to brine.
	Improper curing.	Keep brine at proper strength and the product well covered. Cure until fermentation is complete (bubbles disappear, usually about 6 weeks).
	Long lapse of time between gathering and brining.	Pickling process should be started within 24 hours after gathering.
	Faulty growth of cucumber.	None. During washing, hollow cucumbers usually float. Remove and use for relishes.
Shriveled pickles	Placing cucumbers in too strong brine, heavy syrup, or too strong vinegar.	Use 10-12% brine, amount of sugar called for in recipe, and vinegar that is 5% acidity.
	Long lapse of time between gathering and brining.	Brine within 24 hours after gathering.

continued on next page

Problem	Diagnosis	Remedy
Dark or discolored pickles	Minerals in hard water.	Use soft water.
	Ground spices used.	Use whole spices.
	Spices left in pickles.	Place spices loosely in cheesecloth bag so they can be removed before canning.
	Brass, iron, copper, or zinc utensils used.	Use unbroken enamelware, glass, stainless steel, or stoneware utensils.
Spotted, dull, or faded color	Cucumbers not well cured (brined).	Use brine of proper concentration (10–12% salt). Complete fermentation process (until bubbles disappear).
	Excessive exposure to light.	Store in dark, dry, cool place.
	Cucumber of poor quality.	Work with good quality produce.
Scum on cucumber brines while curing	Wild yeast, molds, and bacteria that feed on the acid thus reducing the concentration of this constituent in brine.	Remove scum as often as needed.

MAKING SAUERKRAUT

You will never have tastier sauerkraut than the batch you make yourself. Kraut can be eaten immediately after it has fermented, or it may be canned, using the boiling water bath method. Sauerkraut is easy to make.

- **25 pounds cabbage**
- **¾ cup Mrs. Wages® Pickling & Canning Salt**

STEP BY STEP INSTRUCTIONS:

1. Remove the coarse outer leaves of heavy, firm heads of cabbage. Wash the heads. Cut the heads into quarters. Cut out the core.

2. Cut 5 pounds of cabbage at a time into shreds no thicker than a quarter. In a large pan, mix 5 pounds of cabbage with 3 tablespoons of Mrs. Wages® Pickling & Canning Salt. Mix well, and then allow to stand for several minutes, until cabbage wilts slightly.

3. Pack the cabbage into a clean jar or crock. Press it down firmly until juice covers cabbage.

4. If container is large enough, add 5 or more pounds of cabbage, repeating Steps 1 through 3. Be sure to leave a minimum of 4 inches of space at the top of the crock. If juice does not cover cabbage, add boiled and cooled brine (1½ tablespoons Mrs. Wages® Pickling & Canning Salt per quart of water).

5. Put a heavy duty, food-safe freezer bag on the cabbage and fill it with water until it sits firmly, allowing no air to reach the cabbage. Close bag securely. Cover container with clean towel.

6. Store at 70 to 75°F, allowing cabbage to ferment for 3 to 4 weeks. At 60 to 65°F, fermentation will take 3 to 6 weeks. Above 75°F kraut may soften.

7. Check it daily. Remove any scum that forms. If brine level becomes low, add 2½% brine (⅓ cup Mrs. Wages® Pickling & Canning Salt to 1 gallon of water). When no bubbles appear, fermentation is complete.

8. To can, put kraut into stockpot and heat to simmering. While still hot, pack into clean, hot jars. Follow instructions for boiling water bath method. Cover with hot juice, leaving ½-inch headspace. Remove bubbles. Wipe rims and adjust lids, then process in boiling water bath canner, pints for 10 minutes, quarts for 15 minutes.

Yield: 9 quarts

Note:
Do not use aspartame sweetener in this recipe.

BREAD AND BUTTER PICKLES WITH ARTIFICIAL SWEETENER

- 4 quarts medium-size pickling cucumbers (about 6 pounds)
- 1½ cups onion slices (about 1 pound)
- 2 large garlic cloves
- ⅓ cup Mrs. Wages® Pickling & Canning Salt
- 1-2 quarts ice (2 trays) crushed or cubes
- artificial sweetener to equal 4½ cups granulated sugar
- 1½ teaspoons turmeric
- 1½ teaspoons celery seed
- 2 tablespoons mustard seed
- 4 cups Mrs. Wages® Pickling & Canning Vinegar or other commercial white vinegar (5% acidity)
- 1 cup water

1. Wash cucumbers thoroughly, using a vegetable brush. Cut ¹⁄₁₆-inch from blossom end. Drain on rack. Slice unpeeled cucumbers into ⅛ to ¼-inch slices. Place in a large bowl. Add onions and garlic. Add salt and mix thoroughly. Cover with crushed ice or ice cubes. Allow to stand for 3 hours. Drain thoroughly. Remove garlic.

2. Combine sweetener, turmeric, celery seed, mustard seed, vinegar, and water. Heat to just a boil. Add cucumbers and onion slices and heat 5 minutes. Pack loosely into clean, hot pint jars. Leave ½-inch headspace. Remove air bubbles and wipe rims. Adjust lids and process in boiling water bath for 10 minutes.

Yield: 7 pints.

PICKLED BEETS

- **4 quarts small beets**

- **3$\frac{1}{2}$ cups Mrs. Wages® Pickling & Canning Vinegar or other commercial white vinegar (5% acidity)**

- **1$\frac{1}{2}$ cups water**

- **2$\frac{1}{4}$ cups granulated sugar**

- **1 tablespoon whole allspice**

- **1$\frac{1}{2}$ teaspoons Mrs. Wages® Pickling & Canning Salt**

- **2 sticks cinnamon**

1. Wash and drain beets. Trim off tops, leaving 1-inch of stem to prevent bleeding. Place beets in a saucepan, cover with water. Bring to boil. Reduce heat and simmer until tender. Drain and discard water. Allow beets to cool.

2. In a large saucepan, combine vinegar, water, sugar, whole allspice, salt, and cinnamon. Mix until the sugar dissolves. Simmer for 10 to 15 minutes. Peel the beets, cut any large beets into quarters, and pack into hot pint jars. Remove cinnamon sticks from the liquid. Bring the liquid to boil. Pour hot liquid over beets, leaving ½-inch headspace. Remove air bubbles and wipe rims. Adjust the lids and process immediately, for 30 minutes using the boiling water bath method.

Yield: 8 pints

BREAD AND BUTTER PICKLES

- **9-11 pounds pickling cucumbers**

- **6³/₄ cups Mrs. Wages® Pickling & Canning Vinegar or other commercial white vinegar (5% acidity)**

- **7 cups granulated sugar**

- **1 package (5.3-ounce) Mrs. Wages® Quick Process Bread and Butter Pickle Mix**

1. Wash cucumbers. Cut off ¹/₁₆-inch from blossom end. Slice cucumbers into ¹/₈-inch slices, and pack the slices into 7 clean, hot quart jars. Combine vinegar, granulated sugar, and Mrs. Wages® Quick Process Bread and Butter Pickle Mix. Stir until the sugar and spices are dissolved. Heat solution to about 180°F. Pour the pickling solution into the 7 jars, being careful to distribute equally among all jars. Complete filling the jars, leaving ½-inch headspace. Use hot vinegar if there is not enough of the pickling solution. Remove air bubbles and wipe rims. Adjust the lids and process immediately for 10 minutes, using boiling water bath method. Use enough water in the canner to cover the jars by 1 or 2-inches.

Yield: 7 quarts

COMPANY-STYLE SWEET PICKLES

- 7 pounds pickling cucumbers
- 1 cup Mrs. Wages® Pickling Lime
- 2 gallons water
- 9 cups granulated sugar
- 1 tablespoon Mrs. Wages® Pickling & Canning Salt
- 2 quarts Mrs. Wages® Pickling & Canning Vinegar or other commercial white vinegar (5% acidity)
- 1 tablespoon celery seed
- 1 tablespoon whole cloves
- 1 tablespoon Mrs. Wages® Mixed Pickling Spice
- 1 cup golden raisins

1. Wash cucumbers and remove $1/16$-inch from blossom end. Slice lengthwise and remove seeds. Mix together pickling lime and water until completely dissolved. Soak cucumbers in lime water for 24 hours (1 cup of lime mixed with 2 gallons water). Remove and rinse well through several changes of cold water to remove all lime sediment. Cover pickles with ice water and let stand 3 hours. Drain well. In a large saucepan, dissolve sugar and salt in vinegar. Place celery seed, whole cloves, and pickling spice in a spice bag. Tie up and place in sugar solution. Bring to boil. Pour hot syrup over pickles and let soak overnight.

2. The next morning, boil pickles in syrup for 30 minutes. Add golden raisins and boil an additional 5 minutes. Remove spice bag. Pack hot pickles into hot jars, leaving ½-inch headspace. Fill jar to within ½-inch top with boiling syrup.

3. Remove air bubbles and wipe rims. Adjust lids and process 10 minutes in a boiling water bath.

Yield: 8 pints

CRISPY PICKLE SLICES

- 4-5 quarts pickling cucumbers, sliced
- 6 cups onion slices
- 2 cups bell pepper slices
- 3 garlic cloves
- 1/3 cup Mrs. Wages® Pickling & Canning Salt
- Cracked ice
- 3 cups Mrs. Wages® Pickling & Canning Vinegar or other commercial white vinegar (5% acidity)
- 5 cups granulated sugar
- 2 tablespoons mustard seed
- 1 1/2 teaspoons turmeric
- 1 1/2 teaspoons celery seed

1. Wash and drain sliced cucumbers. In a large bowl, combine cucumber slices, onions, peppers, garlic, and salt. Cover mixture with cracked ice and let stand for 3 hours at room temperature. Drain well and transfer to a large saucepan.

2. In a separate container, combine vinegar, sugar, mustard seeds, turmeric, and celery seeds. Mix well to dissolve sugar. Pour vinegar mixture over vegetables and bring to boil. Pack into pint jars. Remove air bubbles and wipe rims. Adjust lids and process immediately for 10 minutes, using boiling water bath method. In 24 hours you will have crisp pickle slices.

Yield: 7 to 9 pints

CUCUMBER (MOCK) APPLE RINGS

- 15 large mature pickling cucumbers
- 1 cup Mrs. Wages® Pickling Lime
- 2 gallons water
- 3 cups Mrs. Wages® Pickling & Canning Vinegar or other commercial white vinegar (5% acidity) - divided
- 2 cups water
- 1 tablespoon Mrs. Wages® Alum
- 3 tablespoons red food coloring
- 2 cups water
- 10 cups granulated sugar
- 8 sticks cinnamon

1. Wash, peel, and remove $\frac{1}{16}$-inch from blossom ends of cucumbers. Slice into rings about ¼-inch thick. Remove seeds and soft center from cucumbers. Mix together pickling lime and 2 gallons water. Soak slices 12 to 24 hours or overnight in lime water. Do not use an aluminum container. A food-grade plastic container is acceptable.

2. Discard lime water and rinse slices in cool, fresh water several times to remove any lime residue. Soak 3 hours in fresh ice water. Drain. In a large saucepan, combine cucumber slices and a mixture of 1 cup vinegar, alum, food coloring, and enough water to cover cucumbers. Simmer for 2 hours. Drain and discard liquid. Make syrup with 2 cups vinegar, 2 cups water, sugar, and cinnamon sticks. Bring syrup to a boil. Pour over cucumber slices. Let stand 24 hours.

3. Next day, remove cinnamon. Bring syrup and cucumbers to boil. Pack cucumbers and syrup into hot quart jars, leaving ½-inch headspace. Remove air bubbles and wipe rims. Adjust lids and process 10 minutes in a boiling water bath.

Yield: 6 quarts

DILLS FRESH STYLE

- **10 pounds pickling cucumbers**

- **3⅓ cups Mrs. Wages® Pickling & Canning Vinegar or commercial white vinegar (5% acidity)**

- **7⅓ cups water**

- **1 package (6.5-ounce) Mrs. Wages® Quick Process Dill Pickle Mix**

1. Wash and drain pickling cucumbers cut ¹⁄₁₆-inch from blossom end. Pack into 7 sterilized, hot quart jars. Combine Mrs. Wages® Quick Process Dill Pickle Mix, vinegar and water in a large non-reactive pot. Do not use aluminum. Bring mixture just to a boil over medium heat, stirring constantly until mixture dissolves. Pack cucumbers into hot jars, leaving ½-inch of headspace. Evenly divide hot pickling liquid among the packed jars, leaving ½-inch of headspace. Remove air bubbles and cap each jar as it is filled. If more liquid is needed, heat a mixture of 1 part vinegar to 2 parts water and fill the jars, leaving ½-inch headspace. Remove air bubbles and wipe rims. Adjust lids and process using boiling water bath method.

Pints... 10 minutes

Quarts.. 15 minutes

Yield: 7 quarts

DILL PICKLES OLD STYLE

- **30-40 (5-inch) pickling cucumbers**

- **Fresh dill weed**

- **3 tablespoons Mrs. Wages® Mixed Pickling Spice**

- **8 quarts water**

- **2 cups Mrs. Wages® Pickling & Canning Vinegar or other commercial white vinegar (5% acidity)**

- **1½ cups Mrs. Wages® Pickling & Canning Salt**

1. Wash and dry cucumbers. Cut ¹⁄₁₆-inch from blossom ends. Place a layer of dill weed and about 1½ tablespoons pickling spice in the bottom of a stone, glass, or stainless steel container.

2. Add 30 to 40 (5-inch) cucumbers. Top with another layer of dill weed with the remaining spices. In a large saucepan, combine water, vinegar, and salt. Bring to boil. Cool solution to room temperature. Pour solution over cucumbers, dill, and spices. Weigh the cucumbers down with a weighted plate so all are submerged. Store in a cool, dark place for about 4 weeks. Each day remove any scum that accumulates.

3. At the end of the 4 weeks of curing, check to be sure the pickles are uniformly colored. Discard any that are not. Remove pickles. Strain and boil the curing brine for 5 minutes. Pack pickles into hot jars. Pour boiling hot brine over pickles leaving ½-inch headspace. Remove air bubbles wipe rims. Adjust lids and process immediately, using boiling water bath method.

Pints .... 10 minutes

Quarts .... 15 minutes

Yield: 7 quarts

FRESH PACK PICKLES WITH ARTIFICIAL SWEETENER

- 5 pounds pickling cucumbers
- $1/3$ cup Mrs. Wages® Pickling & Canning Salt
- 4 cups Mrs. Wages® Pickling & Canning Vinegar or other commercial white vinegar (5% acidity)
- 1 cup water
- artificial sweetener to equal 2 cups sugar

1. Wash cucumbers and remove $1/16$-inch from blossom end. Cut cucumbers into thin slices. Combine with salt. Let stand for 1 hour. Drain. Pack drained cucumbers into hot jars.

2. In a saucepan, combine vinegar, water, and sweetener. Bring to boil. Pour boiling brine over cucumbers leaving $1/2$-inch headspace. Remove air bubbles and wipe rims. Adjust lids and process pint jars in boiling water bath for 10 minutes.

Yield: about 6 pints

KOSHER DILLS HOME STYLE

- 50 medium size pickling cucumbers

- 8 heads fresh dill

- 16-24 garlic cloves

- 8 small red or green peppers
  (banana, Hungarian-mild to hot)

- 2 quarts water

- 1 quart Mrs. Wages® Pickling & Canning
  Vinegar or other commercial white vinegar
  (5% acidity)

- 1 cup Mrs. Wages® Pickling & Canning Salt

1. Wash 50 medium-sized pickling cucumbers and remove $\frac{1}{16}$-inch from the blossom ends. Pack whole cucumbers or spears into hot jars. To each jar add 1 head fresh dill, 2 to 3 garlic cloves, and 1 small red or green pepper. In a large saucepan, combine water, vinegar, and salt. Bring to boil. Pour solution over pickles in the jars, leaving ½-inch headspace. Remove air bubbles and wipe rims. Adjust lids and process for 15 minutes, using boiling water bath method. For plain dills, leave out the garlic.

Yield: 8 quarts

Note:

About Lime–Use only food-grade lime. You may use it as a soak for fresh cucumbers 12 to 24 hours before pickling them. Remember, excess lime MUST be removed to make safe pickles. To remove, drain off lime solution, rinse and resoak cucumbers in fresh water for 1 hour. Repeat this process 2 more times. Failure to remove lime may increase risk for botulism.

OLD SOUTH CUCUMBER LIME PICKLES

- **7 pounds medium size pickling cucumbers**
- **1 cup Mrs. Wages® Pickling Lime**
- **2 gallons water**
- **2 quarts Mrs. Wages® Pickling & Canning Vinegar or other commercial white vinegar (5% acidity)**
- **8 cups granulated sugar**
- **1 tablespoon Mrs. Wages® Pickling & Canning Salt**
- **1 tablespoon Mrs. Wages® Mixed Pickling Spice**

1. Wash cucumbers. Remove ¹⁄₁₆-inch from blossom end and slice crosswise. Mix pickling lime in water. Aluminum containers should not be used for the lime solution. Soak cucumbers for 12 hours or overnight in the lime water, stirring occasionally. Rinse 3 times in cool water and soak 3 more hours in ice water.

2. In a bowl, mix together vinegar, sugar, and salt until dissolved. Remove cucumbers from final ice water soak. Drain slices. Pour syrup over top. Let stand for 5 to 6 hours or overnight. Add pickling spice to taste.

3. Drain syrup off cucumber slices into a saucepan. Simmer for 35 minutes. Pack cucumber slices into hot quart jars. Pour boiling syrup over slices to cover and leaving ½-inch headspace. Remove air bubbles. Adjust lids and process pints for 10 minutes and quarts for 15 minutes, using boiling water bath method.

Yield: 5 quarts

QUICK SOUR PICKLES

- About 25 medium size pickling cucumbers
- $\frac{1}{2}$ gallon cider vinegar
- 2 cups water
- $\frac{1}{2}$ cup Mrs. Wages® Pickling & Canning Salt
- $\frac{1}{2}$ cup granulated sugar
- $\frac{1}{2}$ cup mustard seed

1. Wash cucumbers. Remove $\frac{1}{16}$-inch from blossom ends and slice lengthwise. Pack into hot jars. In a large saucepan, mix together vinegar, water, salt, sugar, and mustard seed. Bring to boil. Fill jars to within $\frac{1}{2}$-inch of top with boiling hot liquid. Remove air bubbles and wipe rims. Adjust lids and process for 10 minutes, using boiling water bath method.

Yield: 8 pints

SWEET PICKLES

Use brined pickles that have been desalted. To desalt cucumbers, remove from brine and measure. Submerge in 180 degree water and let stand 4 hours, repeat twice. Lift from final soak and pierce in several places with a fork. Piercing pickles will help prevent shriveling.

- **4 quarts brined, desalted pickles**
- **2 quarts Mrs. Wages® Pickling & Canning Vinegar or other commercial white vinegar (5% acidity)**
- **6 cups granulated sugar, divided**
- **4 teaspoons Mrs. Wages® Mixed Pickling Spice**

1. Pour vinegar into a large stockpot. Add 2 cups sugar and stir well. Tie pickling spice loosely in a cheesecloth bag. Add to stockpot. Bring to boil. Remove the spice bag. Pour the syrup over the pickles, making sure to cover completely. Let stand overnight.

2. The next morning, pour off syrup into a large saucepan. Add 2 cups sugar. Bring syrup to boil. Pour over pickles. On the third day, pour off syrup into a large saucepan. Add 2 cups sugar. Bring syrup to a boil. Pour over pickles. On the fourth day, drain off syrup into a large saucepan and heat it to boil. Pack unheated pickles in clean, preheated jars. Cover pickles with boiling syrup, leaving ½-inch headspace and making certain all pickles are covered. Remove air bubbles and wipe rims. Adjust lids and process for 20 minutes, using boiling water bath method.

Yield: 4 quarts

MRS. WAGES® SPICY PICKLES
MEDIUM OR HOT

- **9-11 pounds pickling cucumbers (about 50 – 3 to 4 inches)**
- **3¹/₃ cups Mrs. Wages® Pickling & Canning Vinegar or other commercial white vinegar (5% acidity)**
- **7¹/₃ cups water**
- **1 pouch Mrs. Wages® Spicy Pickles Mix* (Medium or Hot)**

1. Wash cucumbers and drain. Cut ¹/₁₆-inch slice off blossom end and discard. Leave cucumbers whole, cut into spears or slice.

2. Combine vinegar, water and Mrs. Wages® Spicy Pickles Mix into a large non-reactive saucepan. Do not use aluminum. Bring mixture just to boil over medium heat, stirring constantly until mixture dissolves. Remove from heat.

3. Pack cucumbers into hot jars, leaving ½-inch headspace. Evenly divide hot pickling liquid among the packed jars, leaving ½-inch headspace. Unused brine may be stored in a non-reactive container up to 1 week in refrigerator. Remove air bubbles, wipe rim and cap each jar as it is filled. If more liquid is needed for proper headspace, add a mix of 1 part hot vinegar and 2 parts hot water.

4. Process pints 10 minutes, quarts 15 minutes in a boiling water bath canner. Turn off heat, carefully remove canner lid, and let jars stand for 5 minutes in canner. Remove jars. Let jars sit undisturbed to cool at room temperature for 12 to 24 hours. Test jars for airtight seals according to manufacturer's directions. If jars do not completely seal, refrigerate and consume within 1 week.

5. Product is ready to eat after 24 hours. Before serving, chill to enhance flavor and crispness. Store properly processed shelf-stable product in a cool place, and use within 1 year.

*CAUTION: Due to the spicy nature of this product, irritation of eyes, nose and/or throat may occur during preparation. Care should be taken to avoid inhalation of steam vapors as this could result in irritation and/or coughing. Thoroughly wash skin that comes in contact with the spice. Consult a physician if irritation or coughing persists.

Yield: 7 quarts

WATERMELON RIND PICKLES

- 4 quarts prepared watermelon rind
- 3 tablespoons Mrs. Wages® Pickling Lime
- 2 quarts water
- 8 cups granulated sugar
- 1 quart white Mrs. Wages® Pickling & Canning Vinegar or other commercial white vinegar (5% acidity)
- 1 quart water
- 1 lemon, thinly sliced
- 2 tablespoons whole cloves
- 3 sticks cinnamon (3-inch pieces)
- 2 pieces ginger root (1-inch long)

1. To prepare watermelon rind, trim dark skin and pink flesh from thick watermelon rind. Wash and cut in 1-inch pieces or as desired. Dissolve lime in 2 quarts water in a food grade storage container. Pour over rind. If needed, add more water to cover rind. Let stand for 2 hours at room temperature. Drain and rinse several times to remove all lime. Put rind in a large saucepan and cover with cold water. Bring to boil. Simmer just until tender and drain.

2. Tie cloves, cinnamon, and ginger in cheesecloth bag. In a large saucepan, combine spices with sugar, vinegar, the remaining 1 quart water, and lemon. Simmer for 10 minutes. Add watermelon rind and simmer until rind is clear. Add boiling water if syrup becomes too thick before rind is clear. Remove spice bag. Pack rind into hot jars, leaving ½-inch headspace. Add syrup leaving ½-inch headspace. Remove air bubbles and wipe rims. Adjust lids and process for 10 minutes, using boiling water bath method.

Yield: 7 pints

SOUR PICKLES-MOCK WATERMELON RIND PICKLES

Follow the recipe for Sweet Pickles, eliminating sugar from the liquid poured over the pickles.

Variations between sweet and sour pickles may be made by adding some sugar to the syrup.

- **15 large mature pickling cucumbers**
- **1 cup Mrs. Wages® Pickling Lime**
- **6 cups cider vinegar**
- **10 cups granulated sugar**
- **3 sticks cinnamon**

1. Wash and peel large cucumbers. Remove $\frac{1}{16}$-inch from blossom ends. Cut into 3-inch strips. Remove seeds and soft centers. Place cucumbers in water to cover. Stir in pickling lime. Soak 12 to 24 hours or overnight at room temperature. Discard lime water and rinse cucumbers several times with fresh, cool water. Drain cucumbers well after final rinse. In a large stockpot, combine vinegar, sugar, and cinnamon. Bring to boil, stirring constantly until sugar dissolves. Pour hot syrup over cucumbers and soak for 2 hours. Bring cucumbers and syrup to boil. Simmer gently in syrup mixture for 1 hour or until cucumbers turn clear. Remove cinnamon. Pack cucumbers into hot pint jars. Ladle syrup over top, leaving ½-inch headspace. Remove air bubbles and wipe rims. Adjust lids and process for 10 minutes, using boiling water bath method.

Yield: 10 pints

PICKLED OKRA

- **4 pounds small (2-inches or less) okra pods**

- **5 garlic cloves**

- **3 cups Mrs. Wages® Pickling & Canning Vinegar or other commercial white vinegar (5% acidity)**

- **3 cups water**

- **⅓ cup Mrs. Wages® Pickling & Canning Salt**

- **2 teaspoons dill seed**

- **2-5 hot peppers, chopped, or to taste**

1. Wash okra.

2. Pack okra pods into hot pint jars as tightly as possible. Place a small garlic clove in each jar. In a saucepan combine vinegar, water, salt, dill seed, and hot peppers. Bring mixture to boil. Pour over okra in jars, leaving ½-inch headspace. Remove air bubbles and wipe rims. Adjust lids and process for 10 minutes, using boiling water bath method.

Yield: 5 pints

PICKLED ONIONS

- 4 quarts tiny onions, peeled
- 1 cup Mrs. Wages® Pickling & Canning Salt
- 2 cups granulated sugar
- $1/4$ cup mustard seed
- $2^{1/2}$ tablespoons prepared horseradish
- 2 quarts Mrs. Wages® Pickling & Canning Vinegar or other commercial white vinegar (5% acidity)
- 7 small hot red peppers
- 7 bay leaves

1. To peel onions, cover with boiling water. Let stand 2 minutes. Drain. Dip in cold water and peel. Place onions in large bowl. Sprinkle onions with salt and add cold water to cover. Let stand 12 to 18 hours in refrigerator. Drain, rinse, and drain thoroughly.

2. In a large saucepan, combine sugar, mustard seed, horseradish, and vinegar. Simmer for 15 minutes. Pack onions into hot jars. Add 1 hot pepper and 1 bay leaf to each jar. Bring pickling liquid to boil. Pour over onions, leaving ½-inch headspace. Remove air bubbles and wipe rims. Adjust lids and process for 10 minutes, using boiling water bath method.

Yield: 8 pints

PICKLED PEACHES

- 13 cups granulated sugar

- 8 cups Mrs. Wages® Pickling & Canning Vinegar or other commercial white vinegar (5% acidity)

- 7 sticks cinnamon (2-inch pieces)

- 2 tablespoons whole cloves

- 16 pounds peaches, small or medium

1. In a large saucepan, combine sugar, vinegar, cinnamon, and cloves. (Cloves may be put in a clean cloth, tied with a string, and removed after cooking if not desired in packed product.) Bring to boil. Reduce heat, cover and simmer about 30 minutes.

2. Wash peaches and remove skins. For easy peeling, dip fruit in boiling water for 1 minute. Plunge into cold water. Slip off skins. To prevent prepared peaches from darkening during preparation, immediately place in cold water containing 2 tablespoons of Mrs. Wages® Fresh Fruit Preserver per gallon of water. Drain just before using.

3. Add peaches to boiling syrup, enough for 2 or 3 quarts at a time. Cook for about 5 minutes. Pack hot peaches into clean, hot jars. Continue heating peaches in syrup and packing peaches into jars. Add 1 piece of stick cinnamon and 2 or 3 whole cloves (if desired) to each jar. Cover peaches with boiling syrup to within ½-inch of top. Remove air bubbles and wipe rims. Adjust lids and process for 20 minutes, using boiling water bath method.

Yield: 7 quarts

PICKLED PEPPERS (HUNGARIAN, BANANA, OTHER VARIETIES)

Notes:

- 4 quarts long red, green, or yellow peppers
- 1½ cups Mrs. Wages® Pickling & Canning Salt
- 2 garlic cloves
- 2 tablespoons prepared horseradish
- 10 cups Mrs. Wages® Pickling & Canning Vinegar or other commercial white vinegar (5% acidity)
- 2 cups water
- ¼ cup granulated sugar

1. Wash and drain peppers. Cut 2 small slits in each pepper. In a large container, dissolve salt in 1 gallon water. Pour over peppers and let stand 12 to 18 hours in the refrigerator. Drain. Rinse again and drain thoroughly.

2. In a large saucepan combine garlic, horseradish, vinegar, water, and sugar. Bring to boil. Reduce heat and simmer for 15 minutes. Remove garlic. Pack peppers into hot jars, leaving ½-inch headspace. Pour boiling liquid over peppers in jar leaving ½-inch headspace. Remove air bubbles and wipe rims. Adjust lids and process for 10 minutes, using boiling water bath method.

Yield: 8 pints

JALAPEÑO PEPPERS

- 2 cups jalapeño peppers

- 1 cup Mrs. Wages® Pickling & Canning Vinegar or other commercial white vinegar (5% acidity)

- $\frac{1}{4}$ cup water

- 1 teaspoon Mrs. Wages® Pickling & Canning Salt

- 1 teaspoon Mrs. Wages® Mixed Pickling Spice

1. Wash peppers and pack tightly into hot jar, leaving ½-inch headspace. In a saucepan, combine vinegar, water, salt, and pickling spice. Bring to boil. Pour liquid over peppers leaving ½-inch headspace. Remove bubbles and wipe rim. Adjust lid and process for 10 minutes, using boiling water bath method.

Yield: 1 pint

GREEN TOMATO CRISP PICKLES

- 1 cup Mrs. Wages® Pickling Lime

- 1 gallon water

- 7 pounds green tomatoes

- 8 cups granulated sugar

- 1 gallon Mrs. Wages® Pickling & Canning Vinegar or other commercial white vinegar (5% acidity)

- 1/4 cup Mrs. Wages® Mixed Pickling Spice

- 1 stick cinnamon

- 1 tablespoon Mrs. Wages® Pickling & Canning Salt

1. Stir lime into water, letting any lime that does not dissolve settle to the bottom. Wash, dry, and slice tomatoes into a large crock, glass or food grade plastic container. Do not use aluminum containers. Cover with lime water. Soak for 24 hours at room temperature.

2. Discard lime water. Rinse sliced tomatoes thoroughly in several rinses of cool fresh water. Drain. Mix together sugar and vinegar. Pour over tomatoes. Soak for 12 hours at room temperature. Pour tomatoes and brine into a large saucepan. Tie up pickling spice, cinnamon, and salt in a cloth bag. Add to saucepan. Bring to boil and cook for 30 minutes. Pack tomato slices loosely into clean, hot jars. Remove spice bag and pour hot liquid over tomato slices leaving ½-inch headspace. Remove air bubbles and wipe rims. Adjust lids and process for 10 minutes, using boiling water bath method.

Yield: 7 pints

CRYSTAL PICKLES

- 7 pounds green tomatoes
- 1 cup Mrs. Wages® Pickling Lime
- 2 gallons water
- 2 tablespoons Mrs. Wages® Pickling & Canning Salt
- 9 cups granulated sugar
- 1 teaspoon ground ginger
- 2 quarts Mrs. Wages® Pickling & Canning Vinegar or other commercial white vinegar (5% acidity)
- 6 sticks cinnamon (2-inch pieces)
- 1 teaspoon ground nutmeg

1. Wash and drain tomatoes. Slice green tomatoes ¼-inch thick. Place in porcelain-lined or granite container. Stir lime into water, allowing any lime particles to settle on the bottom. Pour lime mixture over tomatoes. Let stand for 24 hours at room temperature.

2. Discard lime water and rinse tomatoes well through several changes of cold water to remove all lime sediment. Soak in cold water for 4 hours, changing water each hour. Drain. In a large saucepan, combine salt, sugar, and ginger in vinegar. Tie cinnamon and nutmeg loosely in cloth bag. Add to vinegar mixture.

3. Bring to boil. Add tomato slices and boil rapidly until slices are glazed and syrup clings to the spoon in drops. Remove spice bag. Drain syrup into another saucepan and bring to boil. Pack tomato slices loosely into hot jars, leaving ½-inch headspace. Fill jar with boiling syrup to within ½-inch of top. Remove air bubbles and wipe rims. Adjust lids and process for 10 minutes, using boiling water bath method.

Yield: 7 pints

MRS. WAGES® JALAPEÑO PICKLE RELISH

- 6-8 pounds pickling cucumbers
  (about 18 – 3 to 4-inches)

- 1 pound fresh jalapeños
  (about 8 – 3 to 4-inches)

- 2 tablespoons Mrs. Wages® Pickling & Canning Salt

- 2½ cups Mrs. Wages® Pickling & Canning Vinegar or
  other commercial white vinegar (5% acidity)

- 2 cups granulated sugar

- 1 pouch Mrs. Wages® Jalapeño Pickle Relish Seasoning Mix*

1. Wash cucumbers and jalapeños; drain. Cut ¹⁄₁₆-inch slice off blossom end and discard. Cut cucumbers and jalapeños into 1-inch pieces and place in a food processor. Remove and discard jalapeño seeds for more mild relish. Process into small pieces (⅛-inch or smaller is best) and place into a bowl. Stir in salt and mix well. Cover and refrigerate for 2 hours. Drain mixture in a fine strainer to remove excess juice. Do not rinse.

2. Combine vinegar, sugar and Mrs. Wages® Jalapeño Pickle Relish Seasoning Mix into a large non-reactive saucepan. Do not use aluminum. Bring mixture just to boil over medium heat, stirring constantly. Add prepared cucumbers and jalapeños and simmer 10 minutes, uncovered, stirring occasionally. Remove from heat.

3. Ladle hot relish mixture carefully into hot jars, filling evenly. Leave ½-inch headspace. Remove air bubbles, wipe rim and cap each jar as it is filled.

4. Process pints 15 minutes in boiling water bath canner. Turn off heat, carefully remove canner lid, and let jars stand for 5 minutes in canner. Remove jars. Let jars sit undisturbed to cool at room temperature for 12 to 24 hours. Test jars for airtight seals according to manufacturer's directions. If jars do not completely seal, refrigerate and consume within 1 week.

5. Product is ready to eat after 24 hours. Before serving, chill to enhance flavor and crispness. Store properly processed shelf-stable product in a cool place, and use within 1 year.

*CAUTION: Due to the spicy nature of this product, irritation of eyes, nose and/or throat may occur during preparation. Care should be taken to avoid inhalation of steam vapors as this could result in irritation and/or coughing. Thoroughly wash skin that comes in contact with the spice. Consult a physician if irritation or coughing persists.

Yields: 5 pints

CHOW-CHOW RELISH

- 4 cups chopped cabbage
- 3 cups chopped cauliflower
- 2 cups chopped onions
- 2 cups chopped green tomatoes
- 2 cups chopped bell peppers
- 1 cup chopped pimiento
- 3²/₃ cups Mrs. Wages® Pickling & Canning Vinegar or other commercial white vinegar (5% acidity)
- 3 cups granulated sugar
- 3 tablespoons Mrs. Wages® Pickling & Canning Salt
- 2 teaspoons dry mustard
- 1 teaspoon turmeric
- ¹/₄ teaspoon ground ginger
- 2 teaspoons celery seed
- 1 teaspoon mustard seed

1. In a large container combine cabbage, cauliflower, onions, green or just-turning tomatoes, bell peppers, and pimiento or similar peppers. Mix well. Salt lightly and hold in the refrigerator.

2. In a large saucepan combine vinegar, sugar, salt, mustard, turmeric, ginger, celery seed, and mustard seed. Bring to simmer, stirring occasionally. Simmer 5 to 7 minutes. Strain out particulate material. Drain vegetables. Add to brine and simmer 10 minutes. Pack immediately into hot pint jars leaving ½-inch headspace. Add brine to within ½-inch from top. Remove bubbles and wipe rims. Adjust lids and process for 10 minutes, using boiling water bath method.

Yield: 7 pints

CORN RELISH

- 10 cups whole kernel corn
- 2½ cups chopped celery
- 1¼ cups chopped onions
- 2½ cups chopped bell peppers
- 2½ cups chopped sweet red peppers
- 5 cups Mrs. Wages® Pickling & Canning Vinegar or other commercial white vinegar (5% acidity)
- 1¾ cups granulated sugar
- 2½ teaspoons celery seed
- 2½ tablespoons Mrs. Wages® Pickling & Canning Salt
- 2½ tablespoons dry mustard
- 1¼ teaspoons turmeric

Note:
This relish can be made anytime during the year by substituting an equivalent volume of canned whole kernel or frozen corn for the fresh corn.

1. Husk and silk 15 to 20 large ears fresh corn in the late milk stage. Cook for 5 minutes in boiling water and cool quickly in cold water. Drain, blot dry, and cut the whole kernels from the cob. Use 10 cups of whole kernel corn.

2. In a large saucepan combine celery, onions, and peppers. Add vinegar, sugar, celery seed, and salt. Bring mixture to boil. Reduce heat and simmer 5 to 6 minutes. Blend dry mustard and turmeric in ½ cup of simmered mixture. Stir mixture and corn into vinegar mixture. Cook, stirring constantly, for 5 minutes. Pack into hot pint jars, leaving ½-inch headspace. Remove bubbles and wipe rims. Adjust lids and process immediately for 15 minutes, using boiling water bath method.

Yield: 7 pints

PEAR RELISH

- **5-6 pounds pears**
- **3 large bell peppers**
- **3 sweet red peppers**
- **3 large onions, peeled**
- **½ bunch celery**
- **3 cups granulated sugar**
- **5 cups Mrs. Wages® Pickling & Canning Vinegar or other commercial white vinegar (5% acidity)**
- **1 tablespoon Mrs. Wages® Pickling & Canning Salt**
- **1 tablespoon allspice**

1. Wash, peel, and core pears. Remove stems and seeds from peppers. Wash all produce, drain. Process pears, peppers, onions, and celery in a food processor until chopped. Transfer to a large saucepan. Add sugar, vinegar, salt, and allspice. Mix ingredients thoroughly and let stand overnight in the refrigerator.

2. Bring mixture to a boil. Pack mixture while hot into clean, hot jars, leave ½-inch headspace. Remove air bubbles and wipe rims. Adjust lids and process for 10 minutes, using boiling water bath method.

Yield: 9 pints

MRS. WAGES® SWEET PICKLE RELISH

Note:
*Processing time listed is for altitudes less than 1000 feet. At altitudes of 1000 feet or more, increase processing time 1 minute for each 1000 feet of altitude.

- **6-8 pounds pickling cucumbers (about 25 – 3 to 4-inches)**

- **¼ cup Mrs. Wages® Pickling & Canning Salt**

- **2½ cups Mrs. Wages® Pickling & Canning Vinegar or other commercial white vinegar (5% acidity)**

- **2 cups granulated sugar**

- **1 pouch Mrs. Wages® Sweet Pickle Relish Mix**

1. Wash cucumbers and drain. Cut ¹⁄₁₆-inch slice off blossom end and discard. Cut cucumbers into 1-inch pieces and place in a food processor. Process into small pieces (⅛-inch or smaller is best) and place into a bowl. Stir in salt and mix well. Cover and refrigerate for 2 hours. Drain mixture in a fine strainer to remove excess juice. Drain and re-cover vegetables with fresh ice water for another hour. Drain again.

2. Combine vinegar, sugar and Mrs. Wages® Sweet Pickle Relish Mix into a large non-reactive saucepan. Do not use aluminum. Bring mixture just to boil over medium heat, stirring constantly. Add prepared cucumbers and simmer 10 minutes, uncovered, stirring occasionally. Remove from heat.

3. Ladle hot relish mixture carefully into hot jars, filling evenly. Leave ½-inch headspace. Remove air bubbles, wipe rim and cap each jar as it is filled.

4. Process pints 15 minutes in boiling water bath canner. Turn off heat, carefully remove canner lid, and let jars stand for 5 minutes in canner. Remove jars. Let jars sit undisturbed to cool at room temperature for 12 to 24 hours. Test jars for airtight seals according to manufacturer's directions. If jars do not completely seal, refrigerate and consume within 1 week.

5. Product is ready to eat after 24 hours. Before serving, chill to enhance flavor and crispness. Store properly processed shelf-stable product in a cool place, and use within 1 year.

Yield: 5 pints

NOTES

Home Canning

GUIDE AND RECIPES

JELLIES AND JAMS

JELLIES AND JAMS

Jams and jellies are good for all meals, from luscious amounts heaped on hot toast at breakfast to a sparkling dish when served at a formal dinner. They appeal to both children and adults, making meals opportunities to remember the pleasures of gathering the fruit on a hot summer day.

And a jar of jelly, its color contrasting with the bow that decorates the jar, is hard to beat as the most personal of gifts. The Mrs. Wages® Fruit Pectin Home Jell® and Mrs. Wages® Lite Fruit Pectin Home Jell® take much of the guesswork out of jelly-making, and assure you of the finest of results, even if this is your first attempt.

WHAT ARE JAMS, JELLIES AND ALL THE OTHERS?

Jellies are made of fruit juices or other flavored juices and sugar, and are jelled enough to be shimmering firm. No particles of fruit are seen in jellies.

Jams are made from crushed or ground fruit, and have enough jell to hold their shape.

Preserves contain whole fruits or large pieces of fruit in a slightly jellied syrup. Marmalades are clear jellies in which pieces of citrus or other fruits are mixed. Conserves consist of mixed fruits and citrus, with raisins and nuts.

EQUIPMENT FOR MAKING JELLY

You will find you have most of the equipment you need to make jelly.

First, you will need a large saucepan, holding at least 8 quarts, so a mixture can be boiled without fear of boiling over. You can buy the jelly bag you will need for straining out the juice, or you can fashion one out of several layers of cheesecloth. And you will need a bowl to catch the juice.

Other needs: a knife for cutting up the fruit, a large spoon for stirring the mixture, and a timer that will measure one minute accurately. You have a wide choice of containers for jelly. There are standard jars with lids and bands. There are also special jelly/jam jars that range in size from 4-ounces to 12-ounces.

MAKING JELLY

Since many recipe directions call for cooking above boiling point, a jelly/candy thermometer would be helpful.

Follow these steps for making never-fail jelly.

1. Prepare home canning jars and lids according to manufacturer's instructions for sterilized jars. Keep jars hot until filled. Always use new lids.

2. Measure sugar into dry container and set aside.

3. Prepare fruit as directed in the recipe.

4. If making jelly, extract juice by placing prepared fruit in damp jelly bag or use several thicknesses of cheesecloth to form bag. Twist bag together at the top. Squeeze or press gently to increase flow. To improve clarity, filter juice through damp cheesecloth. For clearest juice, double the specified amount of fruit and let juice drop through bag without squeezing. Measure juice with standard liquid measuring cup. If juice yield is slightly short, add water to pulp in bag and squeeze again.

5. Place measured juice or prepared fruit into 6-quart or 8-quart saucepan. Stir in Mrs. Wages® Fruit Pectin Home Jell® and bottled lemon juice, if listed.

6. When mixture comes to a full boil, quickly stir in premeasured sugar amount. Stirring constantly, return to a full boil (a boil that cannot be stirred down) and boil for 1 minute. Do not overcook pectin as it may break down and prevent gelling. Mrs. Wages® Fruit Pectin Home Jell® requires sugar. Sugar is necessary not only for flavor, it preserves and aids in gelling. It is not recommended varying from recipe.

7. Remove from heat and skim off foam. Quickly ladle into hot jars. Leave ¼-inch headspace at the top. Use a clean damp cloth to wipe any spilled jam or jelly from rims and threads of jars. Cover with hot lids and tighten rings firmly.

8. Set hot jars on rack in canner or large saucepot of boiling water. Water must cover jars by 1 or 2 inches. Cover canner and return to boiling. Boil for 5 minutes (begin timer when water has returned to a boil). At altitudes of 1000 feet or higher, increase processing time 1 minute for each 1000 feet of altitude. **THIS STEP IS IMPORTANT.**

9. Remove canner from heat, remove lid and let jars sit 5 minutes in canner. Remove jars from canner, set on a clean towel or rack to cool.

10. When cool, check seals. Lids should be down in the center or stay down when pressed. Label, date and store in a cool, dark, dry place. Unsealed jars should be refrigerated and used within 3 weeks.

IF THE JELLY DOES NOT SET

Your jelly has not jelled or set properly if the contents of the jars are obviously liquid or if the partially jelled contents shift or separate from the sides when the jars are tilted.

There are several reasons why jellies fail to set properly: cooking too long or too slowly, too little acid or pectin, too little sugar, or too much sugar. Sometimes, for no obvious reason, even after you have followed the instructions exactly, jelly will not set properly. Recooking a batch of jelly with a small amount of additional pectin may solve the problem. Unset jelly may be used as pancake or waffle syrup or ice cream topping.

Partially set jelly should be given an extra day after it is made before it is recooked. It may reach an acceptable gel with extra time.

Recook 4 cups of jelly at a time. Mix 4 teaspoons of Mrs. Wages® Fruit Pectin Home Jell® into ¼ cup of water in a large saucepan. Bring the mixture to boiling, stirring constantly to keep it from scorching. Add the jelly and ¼ cup of granulated sugar. Stir thoroughly and bring mixture quickly to a full rolling boil. Boil for 30 seconds, stirring constantly. Remove jelly from heat, skim off foam, pour into sterilized, hot jars, wipe rims and add new lids. Adjust lids and process for 5 minutes, using boiling water bath method.

Remedies for Jelly, Preserves Problems

Problem	Diagnosis	Remedy
Jellies		
Formation of crystals	1. Excess sugar.	1. Test the fruit juice with jelmeter for proper proportions of sugar.
	2. Under dissolved sugar sticking to sides of saucepan.	2. Wipe side of pan free of crystals with damp cloth before filling jars.
	3. Tartrate crystals in grape juice.	3. Make grape juice, pasteurize, and let tartrate crystals settle by refrigerating juice overnight and straining before making jelly.
	4. Mixture cooked too slowly or too long.	4. Cook at rapid boil. Remove from heat immediately when jellying point is reached.

Problem	Diagnosis	Remedy
Jellies (continued)		
Too soft	1. Overcooking fruit to extract juice.	1. Avoid overcooking as this lowers the jellying capacity of pectin.
	2. Incorrect proportions of sugar and juice.	2. Follow recommended instructions.
	3. Undercooked causing insufficient concentration.	3. Cook rapidly to jellying point.
	4. Insufficient acid.	4. Lemon juice is sometimes added if the fruit is acid deficient.
	5. Making too large a batch at one time.	5. Make only one batch of jelly at a time following recipe directions.
Syneresis or "weeping"	1. Excess acid in juice makes pectin unstable.	1. Maintain proper acidity of juice.
	2. Storage place too warm or storage temperature fluctuated.	2. Store in cool, dark, and dry place.
Too stiff or tough	1. Overcooking	1. Cook jelly mixture to temperature of 220° F. or until it "sheets" from a spoon.
	2. Too much pectin in fruit.	2. Use ripe fruit. Decrease amount if using commercial pectin.
	3. Too little sugar, which requires excessive cooking.	3. When pectin is not added use ¾ cup granulated sugar to 1 cup juice for most fruits.
Cloudiness	1. Green fruit (starch).	1. Use firm, ripe, or slightly under ripe fruit.
	2. Imperfect straining.	2. Do not squeeze juice but let it drip through jelly bag.
	3. Juice allowed to stand before it was poured into jars or poured too slowly.	3. Pour into jars immediately upon reaching jellying point. Work quickly.

Problem	Diagnosis	Remedy
Preserves		
Shriveled product	1. Syrup at outset is too heavy for the fruit used.	1. Begin fruit in a syrup thin enough so this will gradually replace the liquid drawn from the fruit, thus they retain original size and shape.
Not a characteristic fruit flavor	1. Overcooked or scorched.	1. Should be stirred frequently when mixture begins to thicken to prevent sticking. Cook only to jellying point.
	2. Inferior fruit used.	2. Select only sound, good flavored fruit.
Tough product	1. Starting fruit in a syrup too heavy.	1. Cook each fruit at first according to directions, then by evaporation; gradually increase the concentration of the syrup as it diffuses into the fruit.
	2. Not plumping fruit properly.	2. Fruit should plump at least 24 hours covered in syrup before being canned.
	3. Overcooking.	3. Cook according to directions.
Sticky, gummy product	1. Overcooking.	1. Follow accepted directions for each product. (Cook only until syrup is quite thick and fruit is fairly translucent.)
Darker than normal in color	1. Cooking too large quantities at a time.	1. It is usually best to cook not more than 2-4 pounds of prepared fruit at a time.
	2. Cooking too slowly.	2. A better color is usually produced if the product is cooked rapidly.
	3. Overcooking sugar and juice.	3. Avoid long boiling. Best to make small quantity of jelly and cook rapidly.
Loss of color	1. Improper storage.	1. Store in a dark, dry, cool place.
Mold or fermentation Do not use	1. Improper sealing.	1. Jars should be sealed airtight.
	2. Failure to process finished product.	2. Processing preserved products in boiling water bath (212°F.) is an added protection against mold or fermentation.
	3. Improper storage.	3. Store in dark, dry, cool place.

APPLE JELLY

- 5 pounds of tart, ripe apples

- 5 cups water

- 2 tablespoons bottled lemon juice

- 1 package Mrs. Wages® Fruit Pectin Home Jell®

- 5½ cups granulated sugar

Note:

Spiced apple jelly may be made by adding a few whole spices to the apples as they are cooking. Added spice should be tied in a cloth bag. Crabapple jelly may also be made following this procedure.

1. Select ripe tart apples. Sort, wash and remove stem and blossoms ends. Do not core. Chop finely. Place in large saucepan, add 5 cups of water, cover and bring to boil. When the mixture starts to boil, reduce heat and simmer about 10 minutes, stirring occasionally. Place apples into a jelly bag. Let the juice drip into a clean pan. Juice yield will be about 4 cups. Add 2 tablespoons of bottled lemon juice to prepared juice. Follow the procedure under making jelly.

Yield: 6 to 7 cups

BLACKBERRY JELLY

- 10-12 cups blackberries

- 1 cup water, if needed

- 1 package Mrs. Wages® Fruit Pectin Home Jell®

- 4½ cups granulated sugar

1. Sort, stem and wash firm ripe blackberries. Crush thoroughly. Place in large saucepan, add 1 cup water, if needed. Cover and bring to a boil. Reduce heat and simmer 5 to 10 minutes or until the berries are soft. Extract juice by placing cooked berries in a jelly bag suspended over a bowl. Juice yield should be about 3½ cups. Follow the procedure under making jelly.

Yield: 5 to 6 cups

CHERRY JELLY

- 3¹/₂ pounds cherries
- ¹/₂ cup water
- 3¹/₂ cups cherry juice
- 1 package Mrs. Wages® Fruit Pectin Home Jell®
- 4¹/₂ cups granulated sugar

1. Discard damaged fruit. Remove stems, wash and crush the fruit without removing the pits. Place in a large saucepan, add ½ cup of water, cover and bring to a boil. Reduce heat and simmer 10 minutes or until the cherries are soft. Place in a jelly bag and extract the juice. Juice yield should be about 3½ cups. Follow the procedure under making jelly.

Yield: 5 to 6 cups

GRAPE JELLY

- 5 pounds muscadine grapes
- ³/₄ cup water
- 1 package Mrs. Wages® Fruit Pectin Home Jell®
- 7 cups granulated sugar

1. Sort, wash, and remove stems and leaves from ripe grapes. Crush one layer at a time. Place crushed grapes in a large saucepan, add ¾ cup water, cover and bring to a boil. Reduce heat and simmer for about 10 minutes, stirring occasionally. Place fruit and liquid in a jelly bag and extract juice. Place juice in a container in the refrigerator overnight. Before making jelly, filter juice through two or more thicknesses of cheesecloth to remove any crystals that may form in the juice. Juice yield will be about 5 cups. Follow the procedure under making jelly.

Yield: 8 cups

GRAPE JELLY
(FROM FROZEN CONCENTRATE)

- 1 can (6-ounce) frozen concentrated grape juice
- 2 cups water
- 1 package Mrs. Wages® Fruit Pectin Home Jell®
- 3³/₄ cups granulated sugar

1. Follow directions for Grape Jelly substituting the above ingredients. Follow the procedure under making jelly.

Yield: 4 cups

MINT JELLY

- 1¹/₂ cups packed mint
- 3 cups water
- 2-3 drops green food coloring
- 1 package Mrs. Wages® Fruit Pectin Home Jell®
- 4 cups granulated sugar

1. Wash mint stems and leaves. Crush or chop finely. Place mint in a saucepan and add 3 cups of water and bring to a boil. Remove from heat, cover and let stand for 10 minutes. Strain through two or more thicknesses of damp cheesecloth. Add 2 to 4 drops of green food coloring, if desired. This will yield 3 cups mint infusion to make jelly. Part of the infusion may be replaced with apple juice for variety. Follow the procedure under making jelly.

Yield: 6 cups

ORANGE JELLY

- 2 cans (6-ounces each) frozen concentrated orange juice

- 1½ cups water

- 1 package Mrs. Wages® Fruit Pectin Home Jell®

- 4½ cups granulated sugar

1. Dilute concentrated orange juice with water. Mix until the orange juice is thawed. Place in a jelly bag and extract the juice. (If you have no objection to a cloudy appearance, omit the juice extraction step and make jelly-jam product with the orange pulp left in.) Juice yield will be about 3 cups. Follow the procedure under making jelly.

Yield: 5 cups

PEACH JELLY

- 3½ pounds ripe peaches

- 1 package Mrs. Wages® Fruit Pectin Home Jell®

- 4½ cups granulated sugar

1. Wash and trim firm, ripe peaches, preferably freestone. Place peaches in a wire-mesh basket and dip them into boiling water for 1½ to 2 minutes. Run cool water over peaches and slip off peel. Cut into pieces, crush, and discard the pits. In a saucepan, bring fruit to boil. Reduce heat and simmer about 10 minutes. Place in a jelly bag and extract the juice. Juice yield will be about 3 cups. Follow the procedure under making jelly.

Yield: 5 to 6 cups

PLUM JELLY

- 4½-5 pounds tart, ripe plums
- 1 cup water
- 1 package Mrs. Wages® Fruit Pectin Home Jell®
- 7 cups granulated sugar

1. Sort and wash plums. Discard damaged fruit. Cut plums into pieces, leaving both the peel and pits in the batch. In a saucepan, crush fruit, add 1 cup water. Cover and simmer for 10 minutes. Place in a jelly bag and extract the juice. Juice yield will be about 5 cups. Follow the procedure under making jelly.

Yield: 8 to 9 cups

RASPBERRY JELLY

- 14 cups firm, ripe raspberries
- ½ cup water
- 1 package Mrs. Wages® Fruit Pectin Home Jell®
- 5½ cups granulated sugar

1. Sort, trim, stem, and wash raspberries. Crush the berries thoroughly. Place in a saucepan, and add ½ cup water. Bring to a boil. Reduce heat and simmer for about 10 minutes, stirring occasionally. Place in a jelly bag and extract the juice. Juice yield will be about 4 cups. Follow the procedure under making jelly.

Yield: 7 to 8 cups

STRAWBERRY JELLY

- 12 cups firm, ripe strawberries
- 1 package Mrs. Wages® Fruit Pectin Home Jell®
- 4½ cups granulated sugar

1. Sort, stem, and wash firm strawberries. Crush thoroughly. Place in a large saucepan, add up to 1 cup water, if needed. Cover and bring to boil. Reduce heat and simmer for 5 to 10 minutes. Place in a jelly bag and extract the juice. Juice yield will be about 3½ cups. Follow the procedure under making jelly.

Yield: 5 cups

MRS. WAGES® PEPPER JELLY

- **4 pounds fresh bell peppers (8-10 medium)***

- **2 cups Mrs. Wages® Pickling & Canning Vinegar or other commercial white vinegar (5% acidity)**

- **¼ cup bottled lemon juice**

- **1 Mrs. Wages® Pepper Jelly Kit****

- **9 cups granulated sugar**

1. Wash bell peppers, seed and chop. Place chopped peppers in a juicer to extract pepper juice into a 2-quart container. Skim off foam. Or, place chopped peppers in a food processor and puree to smooth. Gently strain puree through cheesecloth into a 2-quart container. If needed, add water to pepper juice to yield 5 cups (40 fl oz) of juice.

2. Combine prepared pepper juice, vinegar and lemon juice in a large non-reactive saucepan. Do not use aluminum. Stir in Mrs. Wages® Pectin Blend and Mrs. Wages® Pepper Jelly Mix. Heat mixture to a boil, stirring frequently. Stir in sugar all at once, and return mixture to a full rolling boil. Boil hard for 1 minute, stirring constantly. Remove from heat.

3. Ladle hot mixture carefully into hot jars, filling evenly. Leave ¼-inch headspace. Remove air bubbles, wipe rim and cap each jar as it is filled.

4. Process half-pints 5 minutes in a boiling water bath canner. Turn off heat, carefully remove canner lid and let jars stand for 5 minutes in canner. Remove jars. Let jars sit undisturbed to cool at room temperature for 12 to 24 hours. Test jars for airtight seals according to manufacturer's directions. If jars do not completely seal, refrigerate and consume within 1 week.

5. Product is ready to eat after 24 hours. Before serving, chill to enhance flavor. Store properly processed shelf-stable product in a cool place, and use within 1 year.

   *Please note, combining green bell peppers with red, yellow or orange bell pepper may result in an unappealing jelly color.

   **Included in Mrs. Wages® Pepper Jelly Kit: 1 pouch Mrs. Wages® Pectin Blend and 1 pouch Mrs. Wages® Pepper Jelly Mix.

Yield: 12 half-pints

MAKING JAMS

Making jam is even easier than making jelly because there's no need to extract the juice from the fruit.

HERE ARE THE STEPS:

1. Prepare home canning jars and lids according to manufacturer's instructions for sterilized jars. Keep jars hot until filled. Always use new lids.

2. Wash, trim and prepare fruit as directed in recipe chart.

3. Measure sugar into dry container and set aside.

4. Place measured prepared fruit into 6-quart or 8-quart saucepan. Stir in Mrs. Wages® Fruit Pectin Home Jell® and bottled lemon juice, or butter if listed.

5. Place on high heat stirring constantly. When mixture comes to a full boil, quickly stir in premeasured sugar amount. Stirring constantly, return to a full boil (a boil that cannot be stirred down) and boil for 1 minute. Do not overcook pectin as it may break down and prevent gelling. Mrs. Wages® Fruit Pectin Home Jell® requires sugar. Sugar is necessary not only for flavor, it preserves and aids in gelling. It is not recommended varying from recipe.

6. Remove from heat and skim off foam. Quickly ladle into hot jars. Leave ¼-inch headspace at the top. Use a clean damp cloth to wipe any spilled jam from rims and threads of jars. Cover with hot lids and tighten rings firmly.

7. Set hot jars on rack in canner or large saucepot of boiling water. Water must cover jars by 1 or 2 inches. Cover canner and return to boiling. Boil for 5 minutes (begin timer when water has returned to a boil). At altitudes of 1000 feet or higher, increase processing time 1 minute for each 1000 feet of altitude. **THIS STEP IS IMPORTANT.**

8. Remove canner from heat, remove lid and let jars sit 5 minutes in canner. Remove jars from canner, set on a clean towel or rack to cool.

9. When cool, check seals. Lids should be down in the center or stay down when pressed. Label, date and store in a cool, dark, dry place. Unsealed jars should be refrigerated and used within 3 weeks.

BLACKBERRY OR RASPBERRY JAM

Notes:

- 8 cups blackberries or raspberries
- 1 package Mrs. Wages® Fruit Pectin Home Jell®
- 7 cups granulated sugar

1. Sort, remove the caps, wash, and crush berries. Use as is or if too seedy, sieve part or all of pulp. Measure 5 cups prepared fruit. Follow the procedure under making jam.

Yield: 8 to 9 cups

CHERRY JAM

- 3 pounds sour cherries
- 1 package Mrs. Wages® Fruit Pectin Home Jell®
- 5 cups granulated sugar

1. Sort, trim, and wash cherries. Remove the pits and stems. Chop or coarsely grind cherries. Measure 4 cups prepared fruit. Follow the procedure under making jam.

Yield: 6 cups

FIG JAM

- 3 1/4 pounds figs
- 1 package Mrs. Wages® Fruit Pectin Home Jell®
- 1/2 cup bottled lemon juice
- 1/2 cup water
- 7 1/2 cups granulated sugar

1. Sort out damaged fruit. Remove the stems, peel if desired. Grind or crush figs. Measure 5 cups prepared fruit. Follow the procedure under making jam.

Yield: 9 to 10 cups

PEACH JAM

- 3½ pounds peaches
- 1 package Mrs. Wages® Fruit Pectin Home Jell®
- ⅓ cup bottled lemon juice
- 5 cups granulated sugar

1. Wash, peel, and pit firm ripe peaches. Cut in small pieces and crush. Add ⅓ cup bottled lemon juice. Measure 3¾ cups prepared fruit. Follow the procedure under making jam.

Yield: 6 to 7 cups

PLUM JAM

- 4 pounds plums
- ½ cup water
- 1 package Mrs. Wages® Fruit Pectin Home Jell®
- 8 cups granulated sugar

1. Sort, wash and pit ripe plums. Do not peel. Cut into pieces and crush thoroughly. (The pits may be heated in ½ cup of water a few minutes to ease removal of the pulp.) Place in a saucepan with ½ cup water. Cover and simmer for 5 minutes, stirring occasionally. Measure 6 cups prepared fruit. Follow the procedure under making jam.

Yield: 9 cups

STRAWBERRY JAM

- 12 cups strawberries

- ¼ cup water, if needed

- 1 package Mrs. Wages® Fruit Pectin Home Jell®

- 7 cups granulated sugar

1. Sort, stem, and wash firm, ripe strawberries. Crush thoroughly and add water, if needed. Measure 5 cups prepared fruit. Follow the procedure under making jam.

Yield: 8 to 9 cups

STRAWBERRY JAM (FROM FROZEN FRUIT)

- 3 packages (10-ounces each) frozen strawberries

- 2 tablespoons water

- 1 package Mrs. Wages® Fruit Pectin Home Jell®

- 7 cups granulated sugar

1. Thaw frozen strawberries. Crush fruit and add water. Measure 5 cups prepared fruit. Follow the procedure under making jam.

Yield: 8 to 9 cups

ORANGE MARMALADE

- **3 cups prepared oranges (about 3 medium oranges)**
- **1 cup prepared lemon (about 1 medium lemon)**
- **2½ cups water**
- **1 teaspoon butter**
- **1 package Mrs. Wages® Fruit Pectin Home Jell®**
- **5½ cups granulated sugar**

1. Wash fruit, but do not peel. Cut fruit into very thin slices. Discard seeds. Cut slices into thin strips. Place the prepared fruit into an 8-quart pot. Do not use aluminum. Add the water to the pot, bring to boil. Reduce heat and simmer, covered, for 20 minutes. Stir occasionally. Measure exactly 4 cups prepared fruit. Follow the procedure under making jam.

Yield: about 6 to 7 cups

MUSCADINE GRAPE SYRUP (ICE CREAM TOPPING)

- **2 teaspoons Mrs. Wages® Fruit Pectin Home Jell®**
- **3½ cups granulated sugar**
- **2½ cups Muscadine grape juice**
- **1 cup light corn syrup**

1. Mix 2 teaspoons Mrs. Wages® Fruit Pectin Home Jell® with sugar, and set aside. Pour fruit juice in a saucepan and heat for 2 minutes. Add corn syrup and bring mixture to rolling boil. Add premeasured Mrs. Wages® Fruit Pectin Home Jell® and sugar mixture to juice, stirring constantly. Bring to rolling boil. Boil for exactly 1 minute. Remove from heat, skim, and pour into hot jars. Wipe rims and adjust lids. Process for 5 minutes, using the boiling water bath method.

Yield: 5 half-pint jars

JELLIES AND JAMS
WITH LESS SUGAR

Mrs. Wages® Lite Fruit Pectin Home Jell® could put jelly and jam back on the menu. Mrs. Wages® Lite Fruit Pectin Home Jell® is special fruit pectin that does not require sugar to gel, so you can enjoy the true fruit goodness and fresh fruit taste of jam or jelly made with reduced sugar or with no added sugar. If you prefer, sweeten your jam or jelly with a non-sugar sweetener.

The first time you taste a jelly made with just juice and pectin and no sweetening of any kind-your initial reaction may be negative. Most of us are accustomed to the feel and flavor of a very sweet jelly, and an unsweetened jelly will seem tart and bland by comparison. Extracting juice from sound, ripe, flavorful fruit and using as little water as possible, will add some sweetness and flavor to unsweetened jelly. Unsweetened jam also may be quite tart, but usually will not have a bland taste because none of the flavoring components are left behind as they are when juice is extracted to make jelly.

You may want to sweeten your Mrs. Wages® Lite Fruit Pectin Home Jell® jelly or jam with a non-sugar sweetener. These sweeteners provide sweetness without adding significant increases in carbohydrate or calories. You may have to experiment with the amount of sweetener before you find the amount that suits your taste. We recommend starting with enough sweetener to provide the equivalent sweetness of 1 cup of sugar. Do not substitute non-sugar sweeteners for sugar measure-for-measure.

Mrs. Wages® Lite Fruit Pectin Home Jell® jelly and jam offers much more than just fewer calories. Large amounts of sugar required in regular jelly and jam often overpower the delicate flavors and aromas of our best fruits and berries. To experience true fruit goodness, try reduced sugar jelly and jam made with Mrs. Wages® Lite Fruit Pectin Home Jell®. If your dietary needs permit it, use sugar in your Mrs. Wages® Lite Fruit Pectin Home Jell® recipes — not the 5, 6, or 7 cups required in regular jelly or jam, but 1, 2, or 3 cups. Small amounts of sugar enhance the flavor, clarity, yield, and gel without unduly increasing carbohydrate and calorie content.

PERFECT LIGHT JELLY AND JAM

Jelly and jam made with Mrs. Wages® Lite Fruit Pectin Home Jell® will not be perfect, especially when compared to the high quality jelly or jam you expect from Mrs. Wages® Fruit Pectin Home Jell®. There are three areas where low methoxyl jelly and jam do not quite measure up quality-wise to regular jelly and jam:

1. The sparkling clarity of a well-made regular jelly will be diminished in a Mrs. Wages® Lite Fruit Pectin Home Jell® jelly. Jelly without sugar or sweetened with non-sugar products will be somewhat cloudy. The clarity will be improved if sugar is used. In jams, clarity is not a problem.

2. Jelly and jam made with Mrs. Wages® Lite Fruit Pectin Home Jell® may exhibit some degree of syneresis (weeping), especially after it has been opened and refrigerated. The small amounts of liquid will not affect the flavor or texture and can be absorbed from the jelly surface with a paper towel or can be stirred back into the jam.

3. There also may be a change in texture after refrigeration. You may notice a firmer set and a slight loss of spreadability, more so in jelly than in jam.

A NOTE FOR DIABETICS

While significantly lower in carbohydrates per serving than regular jam or jelly, Mrs. Wages® Lite Fruit Pectin Home Jell® products are not carbohydrate or calorie-free. With the advice of one's physician or diet counselor, appropriate amounts of Mrs. Wages® Lite Fruit Pectin Home Jell® jam or jelly probably can be included in most diabetic diets. The total carbohydrate content of each jam or jelly made with Mrs. Wages® Lite Fruit Pectin Home Jell® will depend on the fruit used and on the type and amount of sweetening agent used.

USING MRS. WAGES®
LITE FRUIT PECTIN HOME JELL®

Cooked Jelly and Jam Instructions with Mrs. Wages® Lite Fruit Pectin Home Jell®

1. Prepare home canning jars and lids according to manufacturer's instructions for sterilized jars. Keep jars hot until filled. Always use new lids.

2. Measure sugar or non-sugar sweetener into dry container and set aside.

3. Prepare fruit as directed in recipe chart.

4. If making jelly, extract juice by placing prepared fruit in damp jelly bag or use several thicknesses of cheesecloth to form bag. Twist bag together at the top. Squeeze or press gently to increase flow. To improve clarity, filter juice through damp cheesecloth. For clearest juice, double the specified amount of fruit and let juice drip through bag without squeezing. Measure juice with standard liquid measuring cup. If juice yield is slightly short, add water to pulp in bag and squeeze again.

5. Place measured juice or prepared fruit into 6-quart or 8-quart saucepan. Stir in Mrs. Wages® Lite Fruit Pectin Home Jell® and bottled lemon juice, if listed. LET MIXTURE SIT 5-10 MINUTES. Then bring to a full boil over high heat, stirring constantly.

6. To add sugar or non-sugar sweetener:
   - If no sugar is used, boil* mixture for 1 minute, stirring constantly. Go to Step 7.
   - If a non-sugar sweetener is used, boil* mixture for 1 minute, stirring constantly. Remove from heat and stir in premeasured non-sugar sweetener. Stir well and go to Step 7.
   - If a sugar is used, add premeasured amount when mixture comes to a full boil*. Return to a full boil and boil for 1 minute, stirring constantly. Go to Step 7.

*Do not overcook pectin as it may break down and prevent gelling. It is not recommended varying from recipe.

7. Remove from heat and skim off foam. Quickly ladle into hot jars. Leave ¼-inch headspace at the top. Use a clean damp cloth to wipe any spilled jam or jelly from rims and threads of jars. Cover with hot lids and tighten rings firmly.

8. Set hot jars on rack in canner or large saucepan of boiling water. Water must cover jars by 1 or 2 inches. Cover canner and return to boiling. Boil for 5 minutes (begin timer when water has returned to a boil). At altitudes of 1000 feet or higher, increase processing time 1 minute for each 1000 feet of altitude. **THIS STEP IS IMPORTANT.**

9. Remove canner from heat, remove lid and let jars sit 5 minutes in canner. Remove jars from canner, set on a clean towel or rack to cool.

10. When cool, check seals. Lids should be down in the center or stay down when pressed. Label, date and store in a cool, dark, dry place. Unsealed jars should be refrigerated and used within 3 weeks.

Please review instructions for preparing cooked jam and jelly, on page 118. Once you have your prepared fruit juice measured, continue with Step 5 under instructions for cooked jam and jelly. Remember, the recipes listed in the chart are for use in preparing jelly using one package Mrs. Wages® Lite Fruit Pectin Home Jell®. Do not double batches or vary from these measurements. Mrs. Wages® Lite Fruit Pectin Home Jell® directions and recipes are not interchangeable with Mrs. Wages® Fruit Pectin Home Jell®

Prepared Fruit Juice (Cups)	Mrs. Wages® Lite Fruit Pectin Home Jell® Package	Non-Sugar Sweetener packets	Sugar (Cups)	YIELD (Cups)
4		0	0	4
4	1	18-24	0	4
4		0	1	4+
5		0	2-3	5-6

TO PREPARE JUICE FOR JELLY

4 pounds, apples or crabapples

Select ripe tart apples. Sort, wash, remove stem and blossom ends. Do not peel or core. Chop finely. Place in large saucepan, add 5 cups water, cover and simmer for 10 minutes. Stir occasionally. Crush thoroughly; simmer for 10 minutes, stirring occasionally.

12 cups blackberries, boysenberries

Sort, stem, and wash fully ripe berries. Crush berries thoroughly, one layer at a time. Place in large saucepan; add 1 cup water, if needed. Cover and bring to a boil. Reduce heat and simmer 5 to 10 minutes.

12 cups blueberries

Sort, stem and wash, firm ripe berries. Crush thoroughly. Place in large saucepan, cover and bring to a boil. Reduce heat and simmer for 5 minutes. Stir occasionally. Add 2 tablespoons bottled lemon juice to measured prepared berry juice.

5 pounds sour cherries

Sort, stem and wash, firm ripe cherries, but do not pit. Crush. Place in large saucepan, add ½ cup water, cover and simmer 10 minutes, stirring occasionally.

4½ pounds Concord grapes

Sort, stem and wash ripe grapes. Crush one layer at a time. Place in large saucepan, add 1 cup water, cover and simmer 10 minutes, stirring occasionally.

5 pounds Muscadine grapes

Sort, stem and wash ripe grapes. Crush one layer at a time. Place in large saucepan, add ¾ cup water, cover and simmer for 10 minutes, stirring occasionally. Extract juice and refrigerate overnight in glass containers. Filter through 2 thicknesses of damp cheesecloth to remove any tartrate crystals that may have formed.

continued on next page

5 pounds peaches
    Wash and pit firm, ripe peaches. Do not peel. Crush or chop finely. Place in large saucepan, add 1 cup water, cover and simmer 10 minutes, stirring occasionally.

5 pounds pears
    Wash, peel, and core ripe pears. Crush or chop finely. Place in large saucepan, add 3 cups of water. Cover and bring to boil. Reduce heat and simmer for 10 minutes. Add 2 tablespoons of bottled lemon juice to prepared juice.

4½ pounds plums
    Sort and wash. Do not peel or pit. Cut into pieces and crush thoroughly. Place in large saucepan, add 1 cup water. Cover and bring to boil. Reduce heat and simmer for 10 minutes. Sweet plums may need ¼ cup bottled lemon juice.

16 cups strawberries
    Sort, stem, and wash firm, ripe strawberries. Crush thoroughly. Place in large saucepan; add 1 cup water, if needed. Cover and bring to boil. Reduce heat and simmer 5 to 10 minutes.

JELLY FROM BOTTLED JUICES

Fresh fruits and berries not in season? Use commercially prepared unsweetened bottled juice for the "Prepared Juice" amounts in our jelly recipe chart. No messy juice preparation, no measuring — just pour into saucepan, and continue with Step 5 of instructions under Cooked Jelly and Jam Instructions.

Prepared Fruit Juice (Cups)	Mrs. Wages® Lite Fruit Pectin Home Jell® Package	Non-Sugar Sweetener packets	Sugar (Cups)	YIELD (Cups)
4		0	0	4
4	1	18-24	0	4
4		0	1	4+
5		0	2-3	5-6

WINE JELLY WITH REDUCED SUGAR

- 4 cups sweet wine, 8.5% alcohol by volume
- 1 package Mrs. Wages® Lite Fruit Pectin Home Jell®
- 2 cups granulated sugar

1. If a wine of 12 percent alcohol is used, reduce the amount of wine to 3 cups. Stir Mrs. Wages® Lite Fruit Pectin Home Jell® into wine and let stand for 5 minutes. Bring mixture quickly to boiling over high heat, stirring constantly. Immediately stir in sugar and return to a full rolling boil, stirring constantly. When boiling, remove from heat and skim foam. Pour into sterilized, hot half-pint jars, leaving ½-inch headspace. Wipe rims and adjust lids. Process for 5 minutes in a boiling water bath.

Yield: about 4½ cups

Please review instructions for preparing cooked jam and jelly, on page 118. Once you have your prepared fruit measured, continue with Step 5 under instructions for cooked jam and jelly. Remember, the recipes listed in the chart are for use in preparing jam using one package Mrs. Wages® Lite Fruit Pectin Home Jell®. Do not double batches or vary from these measurements. Mrs. Wages® Lite Fruit Pectin Home Jell® directions and recipes are not interchangeable with Mrs. Wages® Fruit Pectin Home Jell®.

Preparation for jam using Mrs. Wages® Lite Fruit Pectin Home Jell®							
To Make	To Prepare Fruit for Jam	Amount of Fruit	Prepared Fruit (Cups)	Mrs. Wages® Lite Fruit Pectin Home Jell® Package	Non-Sugar Sweetener packets	Sugar (Cups)	YIELD (Cups)
Apricot	Wash, peel and pit, firm ripe apricots. Cut into small pieces and crush. Add ¼ cup bottled lemon juice for 5 cups. For 6 cups crushed apricots, add ⅓ cup bottled lemon juice.	4 lbs.	5 5 5 6	1	0 18-30 0 0	0 0 1-3 3-4	5 5 5-6 7-8
Blackberry Raspberry Boysenberry Dewberry	Sort, stem and wash firm, ripe berries. Crush thoroughly. Sieve all or part of pulp to remove seeds, if desired.	8 cups	4 5	1	24-36 0	0 1-3	4 5-6
Blueberry	Sort, stem and wash firm, ripe berries. Crush thoroughly. Add 2 tablespoons bottled lemon juice.	8 cups	4 4 5	1	0 18-30 0	0 0 1-3	4 4 5-6
Sour Cherry	Sort, stem, wash and pit cherries. Crush or chop finely.	3½ lbs.	4 5	1	24-36 0	0 1-3	4 5-6
Fig	Sort, wash and remove stem ends from figs. Peel, if desired. Grind or crush thoroughly. If using sugar, add ½ cup bottled lemon juice and ½ cup water. If using non-sugar sweetener, add ¼ cup bottled lemon juice and ¼ cup water.	3¼ lbs.	4 4 5	1	0 24-36 0	0 0 1-3	5 5 5-7
Grape (Concord)	Sort, wash and remove stems from ripe grapes. Slip skins from grapes. Place in a large saucepan, add 1 cup of water to pulp. Cover and simmer 5 minutes, stirring occasionally. Sieve pulp to remove seeds. All or part of finely chopped or ground skins may be added to pulp, if desired.	4¼ lbs.	4 4 5	1	0 24 0	0 0 1-3	4 4 5-6
Peach	Wash, peel and pit firm, ripe peaches. Cut into small pieces and crush. Add ¼ cup bottled lemon juice. For 6 cups crushed peaches, add ⅓ cup bottled lemon juice.	4 lbs.	5 5 5 6	1	0 18-30 0 0	0 0 1-3 3-4	5 5 5-6 7-8
Pear	Wash, peel and core ripe pears. Crush or chop finely. Add 2 tablespoons bottled lemon juice for 4 cups crushed pears. Add ¼ cup bottled lemon juice for 5 cups crushed pears. For 6 cups crushed pears, add ⅓ cup of bottled lemon juice.	4-5 lbs.	4 4 5 5	1	0 18-24 0 0	0 0 1-3 2-3	4 4 5-6 6-7

continued on next page

Mrs. Wages Home Canning Guide

Preparation for jam using Mrs. Wages® Lite Fruit Pectin Home Jell®							
To Make	To Prepare Fruit for Jam	Amount of Fruit	Prepared Fruit (Cups)	Mrs. Wages® Lite Fruit Pectin Home Jell® Package	Non-Sugar Sweetener packets	Sugar (Cups)	YIELD (Cups)
Plum	Sort, wash and pit ripe, tart plums. Do not peel. Cut into pieces and crush thoroughly. Add ½ cup water, cover and simmer 5 minutes, stirring occasionally.	4 lbs.	4 5	1	24 0	0 1-3	4 5-6
Strawberry	Sort, stem and wash firm ripe strawberries. Crush thoroughly. Add ¼ cup water, if needed.	12 cups	5 5 5 6	1	0 18-24 0 0	0 0 1-3 2-3	5 5 5-6 6-7

LIGHT HOME-JELL FREEZER JAM

This recipe may be used to make freezer jam with most of the fruits and berries commonly used to make jams: apricots, blackberries, blueberries, peaches or strawberries.

- **3 cups crushed fruit**

- **1 package Mrs. Wages® Lite Fruit Pectin Home Jell®**

- **1 cup granulated sugar**

- **1 cup water**

1. Measure 3 cups crushed fruit at room temperature into a mixing bowl and set aside to use later. Mix together Mrs. Wages® Lite Fruit Pectin Home Jell® and sugar. Stir this mixture into water in a small saucepan.

2. Bring to boil, stirring constantly to prevent scorching or sticking. Boil for 1 minute. Immediately stir hot pectin-sugar mixture into crushed fruit. Stir thoroughly for about 3 minutes.

3. Pour into clean freezer containers, leaving ½-inch headspace. Cover with tight-fitting lids and refrigerate about 3 hours until jam is set. Transfer to freezer. Freeze up to 1 year.

Note:

To make freezer jam without sugar or jam sweetened with a non-sugar sweetener, follow these instructions but omit the sugar. Stir in Mrs. Wages® Lite Fruit Pectin Home Jell® into the water slowly but thoroughly to prevent lumping. To use a non-sugar sweetener, stir 18 to 20 packets (to taste) into the crushed fruit.

MRS. WAGES® LIQUID FRUIT PECTIN

Before You Begin:

• PREPARE and PROCESS home canning jars and lids according to manufacturer's instructions for sterilized jars.

• Keep jars hot until filled.

• Select fresh, firm, ripe fruit at the peak of flavor. Discard under ripe or defective pieces.

• Wash fruit and berries in a colander under cold running water.

• Use only commercially bottled lemon juice.

• Use full amount of sugar called for in the recipe chart. Reducing the sugar may prevent gelling.

• To ensure best results, do not alter the recipes in any way.

• Doubling recipes is not suggested as the product may not set.

• Keep in mind that your jams or jellies could take up to two weeks to set.

• Process jams and jellies in a boiling water bath canner.

• After processing, do not attempt to retighten the bands on the jars as this may crack the seal.

• Liquid and powdered pectin are not interchangeable.

You will need:

• Measuring cups and spoons

• Jelly bag or cheesecloth

• Large metal spoon or skimmer

• 6-quart to 8-quart or larger saucepan

• Colander

• Timer

• Jar funnel, jar lifter, tongs

• Canning jars with 2-piece lids (lids and rings)

• Water bath canner or other large metal container with rack and cover

JELLY FROM BOTTLED JUICES

Fresh fruits and berries not in season? Use commercially prepared unsweetened bottled juice, for the "Prepared Juice" amounts in our jelly recipe chart. No messy juice preparation, no measuring — just pour into saucepan, and continue with Step 5 of instructions under Cooked Jelly and Jam Instructions.

COOKED JELLY AND JAM INSTRUCTIONS WITH MRS. WAGES® LIQUID FRUIT PECTIN

1. Prepare home canning jars and lids according to manufacturer's instructions for sterilized jars. Keep jars hot until filled. Always use new lids.

2. Measure sugar into dry container and set aside.

3. Prepare fruit as directed in recipe chart.

4. If making jelly, extract juice by placing prepared fruit in damp jelly bag or use several thicknesses of cheesecloth to form bag. Twist bag together at the top. Squeeze or press gently to increase flow. To improve clarity, filter juice through damp cheesecloth. For clearest juice, double the specified amount of fruit and let juice drip through bag without squeezing. Measure juice with standard liquid measuring cup. If juice yield is slightly short, add water to pulp in bag and squeeze again.

5. Place measured juice or prepared fruit into 6-quart or 8-quart saucepan. Stir in water and bottled lemon juice, if listed.

6. Stir measured sugar and ½ teaspoon of butter* into prepared fruit in saucepan. Then bring mixture to a full boil over high heat, stirring constantly. *Optional: butter will reduce foaming.

7. Stir in pectin quickly and return to a full boil. Boil <u>exactly</u> 1 minute, stirring constantly. **Do not overcook pectin as it may break down and prevent gelling. It is not recommended varying from recipe.**

8. Remove from heat and skim off foam. Quickly ladle into hot jars. Leave ¼-inch head space at the top. Use a clean damp cloth to wipe any spilled jam or jelly from rims and threads of jars. Cover with hot lids and tighten rings firmly.

9. Set hot jars on rack in canner or large saucepan of boiling water. Water must cover jars by 1 or 2 inches. Cover canner and return to boiling. Boil jelly for 5 minutes and jam 10 minutes (begin timer when water has returned to a boil). At altitudes of 1000 feet or higher, increase processing time 1 minute for each 1000 feet of altitude. **THIS STEP IS IMPORTANT.**

continued on next page

10. Remove canner from heat, remove lid and let jars sit 5 minutes in canner. Remove jars from canner, set on a clean towel or rack to cool.

11. When cool, check seals. Lids should be down in the center or stay down when pressed. Label, date and store in a cool, dark, dry place. Unsealed jars should be refrigerated and used within 3 weeks.

FREEZER JAMS AND JELLY INSTRUCTIONS

1. Use plastic freezer containers or jars with tight fitting lids. Wash, rinse and immerse containers and lids briefly in very hot water or very hot dishwasher rinse. Prepare fruit as directed in recipe chart and measure into large mixing bowl. For best results, crush berries with a potato masher or pulse slightly in a food processor. Do not purée.

2. Measure sugar into a separate bowl. Stir sugar into prepared fruit or juice, and mix well. Stir occasionally for about 10 minutes.

3. Meanwhile, stir Mrs. Wages® Liquid Fruit Pectin into water and lemon juice, if applicable, in a small bowl. Stir pectin mixture into fruit mixture and continue stirring constantly for about 3 minutes or until sugar is completely dissolved.

4. Ladle jam or jelly into containers, leaving ½-inch head space at top. Cover containers and let stand at room temperature up to 24 hours or until set. After jam has set, transfer to freezer.

5. Store in freezer up to 1 year. Once a container is opened, keep in refrigerator and use within a few days.

IMPORTANT: MRS. WAGES® LIQUID FRUIT PECTIN DIRECTIONS FOR USE AND RECIPES ARE NOT INTERCHANGEABLE WITH MRS. WAGES® FRUIT PECTIN HOME JELL® OR MRS. WAGES® LITE FRUIT PECTIN HOME JELL®.

Mrs. Wages® Liquid Fruit Pectin						
COOKED JELLY						
To Make	To Prepare Fruit for Jelly	Amount of Fruit	Prepared Fruit Juice (Cups)	Sugar (Cups)	Mrs. Wages® Liquid Fruit Pectin	Approximate Yield (Cups)
Blueberry	Sort, stem and wash firm ripe berries. Crush thoroughly. Place in large saucepan; add 2 cups water. Bring to a boil. Reduce heat, simmer uncovered 45 minutes, stirring occasionally.	4 cups	4	6	1 pouch	7
Cherry	Sort, stem, wash and pit cherries. Crush or chop finely. Place in large saucepan; add ¾ cup water. Bring to boil. Reduce heat, cover and simmer 10 minutes, stirring occasionally.	3½ lbs	3½	7	2 pouches	8
Grape (Concord)	Sort, stem and wash firm rip grapes. Slip skins from grapes, and crush. Place in large saucepan; add ½ cup water. Bring to a boil. Reduce heat, cover and simmer 10 minutes, stirring occasionally. *Recipe option: Instead of fresh grapes, use unsweetened, commercial 100% grape juice.	*3 lbs	4	7	1 pouch	8
Strawberry	Sort, stem and wash firm ripe berries. Crush thoroughly. Place in large saucepan; add ¼ cup bottled lemon juice. Bring to a boil. Reduce heat, cover and simmer 5 to 10 minutes, stirring occasionally.	12 cups	3¾	7½	2 pouches	9
Blackberry & Apple	Sort, stem, and wash firm rip blackberries. Crush thoroughly. Place in large saucepan; add ⅔ cup water. Bring to boil. Reduce heat, cover and simmer 5 minutes, stirring occasionally. Stem, remove blossoms, and wash apples (do not peel or core). Cut in small pieces. Place in large saucepan; add just enough water to cover. Bring to boil. Reduce heat, cover and simmer for 20 minutes or until apples are tender, stirring occasionally. Combined juice should equal 2 cups. Add 2 tablespoons bottled lemon juice to prepared juice. *Recipe option: Instead of fresh apples, use unsweetened, commercial 100% apple juice.	Blackberries: 1½ lbs *Apples: 4 medium	2	4	1 pouch	6

continued on next page

COOKED JAM

To Make	To Prepare Fruit for Jam	Amount of Fruit	Prepared Fruit (Cups)	Sugar (Cups)	Mrs. Wages® Liquid Fruit Pectin	Approximate Yield (Cups)
Blueberry	Sort, stem and wash, firm rip berries. Crush thoroughly. Add 2 tablespoons bottled lemon juice to prepared fruit.	8 cups	4½	7	2 pouches	10
Peach	Wash, peel and pit firm ripe peaches. Cut into small pieces and crush. Add ¼ cup bottled lemon juice to prepared fruit.	3 lbs	4	7 ½	1 pouch	9
Strawberry	Sort, stem and wash firm ripe strawberries. Crush thoroughly. Add ¼ cup bottled lemon juice to prepared fruit.	12 cups	4	7	1 pouch	12
Apricot & Pineapple	Wash, pit (do not peel) firm rip strawberries. Crush thoroughly. Add ¼ cup bottled lemon juice to prepared fruit. Recipe option: Instead of fresh pineapple, crushed, drained commercial canned may be used.	Apricots: 2½ lbs Pineapple: ½ medium fully ripe	Apricots: 3 Pineapple: 1	7	1 pouch	8
Orange Berry	Sort, stem and wash firm rip berries. Crush thoroughly. Add finely chopped orange segments, 2 Tbsp bottled lemon juice, and 4 Tbsp grated orange peel to prepared fruit.	Blueberries: 2 cups Raspberries: 3 cups Orange segments: ½ cup	5½	6½	1 pouch	8

FREEZER JAM

To Make	To Prepare Fruit for Jam	Amount of Fruit	Prepared Fruit (Cups)	Sugar (Cups)	Mrs. Wages® Liquid Fruit Pectin	Approximate Yield (Cups)
Blueberry	Sort, stem and wash firm ripe berries. Crush thoroughly.	4 cups	2	4	1 pouch	5
Peach	Wash, peel and pit firm ripe peaches. Cut into small pieces and crush. Combine pectin and ¼ cup bottled lemon juice in a small bowl.	2 lbs	3	6	2 pouches	8
Strawberry	Sort, stem and wash firm ripe strawberries. Crush thoroughly. Combine pectin and 2 tablespoons bottled lemon juice in a small bowl.	4 cups	2	4	1 pouch	5

FREEZER JELLY

To Make	To Prepare Fruit for Jam	Amount of Fruit	Prepared Fruit (Cups)	Sugar (Cups)	Mrs. Wages® Liquid Fruit Pectin	Approximate Yield (Cups)
Grape	Place unsweetened, commercial 100% grape juice in a large bowl. Combine pectin and 2 tablespoons water in a small bowl.	2 cups	2	4	1 pouch	5

mrs.wages®

Home Canning

GUIDE AND RECIPES

FREEZING

FREEZING FOODS

If you have the freezer space, freezing food is another option for food preservation. Freezing maintains optimal nutrient retention when food is frozen soon after harvest, vegetables are blanched, and proper storage containers are used. Freezing is easy and works well when you have smaller quantities of food to preserve for later enjoyment.

The end quality of frozen food depends on several factors including what you are freezing (fruit, vegetable, meat, etc.), the variety of the produce, how quickly the food is frozen after harvest, temperature of the freezer, packaging materials, and how long the food is held in the freezer. As in all food preservation, freezing will not improve the quality of the food you are processing — if you start with poor quality food, you will end up with poor quality frozen food.

Food placed in a freezer must be frozen quickly; therefore, it is important that you not overload your freezer. No more than 2 to 3 pounds of unfrozen food per cubic foot of freezer space should be added to the freezer. It will take food approximately 24 hours to freeze, so you will need to plan how much food you can successfully add to your freezer. For example, if you have a 15 cubic foot freezer, plan to add no more than 30 to 45 pounds of food in a 24 hour period. Less food than that will increase the freezing rate and result in a better frozen product.

Also allow space around the packages of food to make the food freeze faster. Once frozen, the packages of food may be stacked.

While freezing food as a method of food preservation is easy, there are some changes that occur in the food during freezing. For this reason, foods that have high water content may be mushy when thawed because the cells of water expand and burst during the freezing process. In addition, fats may oxidize during the freezing process, which may make meats have a rancid or stale flavor.

To help avoid some of the color, flavor, and nutritional losses that occur during the freezing of vegetables, blanching these foods is recommended. Packing fruits in sugar or syrup will also help maintain flavor and color of these foods.

BLANCHING FOR BEST QUALITY

Blanching consists of exposing fruits or vegetables to a very short heat treatment to inactivate natural enzymes that cause undesirable changes.

Most vegetables to be frozen should be blanched first. Fruits, however, are rarely blanched. Disadvantages of blanching fruits exceed benefits. Even though fruits and vegetables are of similar botanical origin their inherent chemistries are different.

Blanching is accomplished by exposing the product to boiling water (immersion), live steam (produce in basket over boiling water using traditional range-top methods), or using microwave energy to heat both water and produce. Vegetables are blanched for a specific amount of time depending on the size of the pieces and the density of the food. Vegetables are then removed from the heat and plunged into ice water to halt the cooking process. The end product is a partially cooked vegetable that is then drained, packaged with little air in the package, labeled, and frozen.

PACKAGING FOR FREEZING

Materials used for freezing foods should be moisture and vapor resistant. These include glass, rigid plastic, metal, heavy aluminum foil, freezer bags, and wrapping materials including freezer paper and films. Freezer tape is available to help achieve an airtight seal. Bags should be no larger than ½-gallon and preferably of a size that holds the amount of food your family will consume in one meal.

Glass and food grade plastic materials are frequently used for freezing foods. Wide-mouth glass jars manufactured specifically for freezing are available. While glass is an excellent material for freezing food, breakage is always a concern. Plastic freezer bags work well but may be difficult to stack in the freezer. Do not use margarine, whipped topping, and other similar type containers for freezing foods.

If you choose to reuse these materials for freezing foods, it is suggested that you line them with a freezer bag before adding food to them.

No matter what you use for freezing your produce, make sure that you can remove most of the air from the package and that you get a good seal to prevent air from damaging the produce. Today there are several companies manufacturing vacuum sealers for food storage. These are excellent for removing air from packaging and for storing foods — they are fairly expensive to purchase so consider how much you will use it before purchasing.

PREPARING FRUITS FOR FREEZING

Fruits to be frozen should be firm and ripe. Under-ripe fruit may have a green, bitter, or off-flavor after freezing. Pick berries when ripe and freeze them as soon after picking as possible. Some fruits-apples, peaches and pears-may need to ripen further (1-2 days) after harvesting. Frozen fruit prepared from overripe fruit will lack flavor and have a mushy texture.

Wash small quantities of fruit gently in cold water. Drain fruit thoroughly. Peel fruit and remove pits and seeds. Halve, slice, chop, crush or purée fruit as indicated in the instructions for each specific fruit. Some fruits, especially berries, may be left whole; remove stems or hulls. Work with small quantities (2-3 quarts) of fruit at a time, particularly if it is fruit that darkens rapidly.

Pack fruit using syrup pack, sugar pack, or unsweetened pack. Most fruit has better texture and flavor when packed with syrup. Apples, berries, grapes, peaches, persimmons, and plums can be frozen satisfactorily without sweetening, but the quality is not as good as freezing in syrup or sugar. Some fruits such as gooseberries, currants, cranberries and rhubarb give a good quality product without sugar.

Anti-Darkening

Many fruits darken during freezing, particularly if not kept under liquid. Darkening occurs when the fruit is exposed to air. Since a small amount of air is in the liquid as well as the tissues of fruit, some darkening can occur even when the fruit is submerged in liquid. To help retard darkening during freezer storage, add Mrs. Wages® Fresh Fruit Preserver according to the package directions.

Syrup Pack

Sugar syrup is made by dissolving sugar in boiling water. Forty percent syrup (3 cups sugar to 4 cups water is 40% sugar by weight) is recommended for freezing most fruits. Syrups containing less sugar are sometimes used for mild-flavored fruits; those with more sugar are used for very sour fruits. The type of syrup to use is specified in the directions for freezing each fruit. Allow ½ to ⅔ cup of syrup for each pint of fruit. Cut fruit directly into the freezer container, leaving the recommended headspace. Add **chilled** syrup to cover fruit.

Syrups for Freezing Fruits

Type of Syrup	Sugar, cups	Water, cups	Yield, cups
10% syrup	½	4	4½
20% syrup	1	4	4¾
30% syrup	2	4	5
40% syrup	3	4	5½
50% syrup	4¾	4	6½
60% syrup	7	4	7¾

To make the syrup, dissolve the sugar in boiling water; stir until the solution becomes clear. Cool and store in the refrigerator until needed.

Pectin syrup (with sugar)

A lighter syrup made with pectin may be used to prepare syrups for freezing berries, cherries, and peaches. With pectin, less or no sugar is needed, and fresh-fruit flavor, color, and texture are retained. Pectin syrup with sugar is prepared as follows:

Mix 1 package of Mrs. Wages® Fruit Pectin Home Jell® with 1 cup of water in a saucepan. Boil for 1 minute. Add ½ cup sugar and stir to dissolve. Remove from heat and pour into a 2-cup glass measure; add enough water to make 2 cups of syrup. Chill. When ready to use, pour a small amount over fruit to form a thin film. Package, seal, and freeze fruit. Two cups of pectin syrup will cover about 16 pints of berries.

Ascorbic acid pack

Dissolve ¼ teaspoon Mrs. Wages® Fresh Fruit Preserver in ¼ cup cold water. Sprinkle over 1 quart (⅞ pound) of fruit.

Quantity of Fresh Fruit Required Per Pint of Frozen Fruit

Fruits	Pounds Fresh/Pint Frozen	Selection
Apples	1¼ to 1½	Tart and sweet, juicy, crisp
Apricots	⅔ to ⅘	Firm, well colored, mature
Berries, except raspberries	1	Well ripened, sweet, uniform color
Cantaloupe	1	Firm, but well ripened
Cherries, all types	1¼ to 1½	Bright, uniform color, mature
Cranberries	½	Firm, mature
Currants	¾	Firm, mature
Peaches	1 to 1½	Firm, ready to eat
Pears	1 to 1½	Ripened, ready to eat
Pineapple	1¼	Firm, fully ripe
Plums	1 to 1½	Mature, deep colored
Raspberries	⅔	Firm, ripe, ready to eat
Rhubarb	⅔	Young, tender, well-colored

Preparing Fruit for the Freezer

Fruits	Preparation	Pre-Treatment and Sweetening
Applesauce	Wash, core, slice; peel if desired. Cook slowly until soft. Strain if desired.	Add sugar to taste. Mix and pack.

continued on next page

Preparing Fruit for the Freezer (continued)

Fruits	Preparation	Pre-Treatment and Sweetening
Apples (for pie – use firm, tart, winter apples)	Wash, pare, core; keep fruit under water until sliced. Spread slices in pan. Steam 2 minutes, depending on apple variety. Cool in very cold water. Drain.	Cover all surfaces with sugar, using about ½ cup for every 4 cups sliced apples.
Berries (except raspberries)	Sort, wash, drain. Steam 1 minute and cool at once.	**Syrup pack:** cover with 30% syrup. **Dry pack:** add ½ cup dry sugar to 1 quart (1⅓ pounds) fruit.
Cantaloupe	Cut in half, remove seeds and rind. Slice, cube or cut balls with ball cutter into cold syrup.	Use 30% syrup.
Cherries, all types	Stem, sort, and wash thoroughly. Drain and pit.	**Syrup pack:** cover cherries with 50% syrup. **Dry pack:** add ⅔ cup sugar to 1 quart (1⅓ pounds) cherries.
Cranberries	Stem, wash, remove soft berries.	No sugar or syrup needed; 50% syrup may be used. Crushed or puréed berries: add 2 cups sugar/quart of berries.
Currants	Wash and remove stems.	Add ½ cup dry sugar to each quart (1⅓ pounds) fruit. Stir until sugar is dissolved.
Peaches	Wash, pare with stainless steel knife. Slice directly into syrup or mix at once with dry sugar.	**Syrup pack:** 30% syrup plus ascorbic acid ½ teaspoon/quart of syrup. **Sugar pack:** dissolve ¼ teaspoon ascorbic acid* in ¼ cup water. Sprinkle over 1 quart of fruit. Add ½ cup sugar/ quart (1⅓ pounds) fruit. **Water pack:** cover peaches with water containing ascorbic acid* ½ teaspoon /quart.
Pears	Wash, peel, cut in halves or quarters and core.	Heat in boiling 30-40% syrup for 1-2 minutes; drain and cool; pack and cover with syrup. Add ascorbic acid* scant ¼ teaspoon (quart) if desired.
Pineapple	Pare, core, and remove eyes. Slice, dice or cut in wedges.	**Syrup pack:** 30% syrup. **Sugar pack:** 1 pound sugar/ 4 pounds fruit. Pineapple juice can be used in place of water (in syrup).
Plums	Wash, sort, drain and cut in halves and pit.	Cover with 40% syrup containing ½ teaspoon ascorbic acid/quart syrup.

Fruits	Preparation	Pre-Treatment and Sweetening
Raspberries	Sort and remove leaves and stems. Wash in cold water. Handle as little as possible.	**Syrup pack:** 40% syrup. **Dry pack:** (for jam or pie). ½ cup sugar/1 quart (1⅓ pounds) fruit. Crushed or puréed fruit: add ¾ cup sugar/quart of fruit.
Rhubarb	Wash, trim, cut in 1-inch pieces. Pack raw or cooked and sweetened.	Pack without sugar or with 30% syrup if desired.
Strawberries	Wash, sort, hull and drain. Work quickly. Slice or leave whole.	**Syrup pack:** 40% syrup. **Sugar pack:** ⅔ cup sugar/quart (1½ pounds berries). **Water pack:** Cover with water containing ½ teaspoon ascorbic acid/quart of water. **Crushed puréed berries:** ⅔-cup sugar/1 quart purée (2 pounds).

Note: Mrs. Wages® Fresh Fruit Preserver may be used. For correct amounts, check package directions.

PREPARING VEGETABLES FOR FREEZING

Select vegetable varieties suitable for freezing. Harvest vegetables such as asparagus, broccoli, corn, peas, snap beans, and lima beans at peak of maturity and plan to freeze them the same day they are picked. If you can't freeze the vegetables immediately after harvest, refrigerate them for a short period of time.

When preparing vegetables, wash a small quantity gently in several changes of cold water. Lift the vegetables out of the water each time so dirt settles to the bottom of the sink or pan.

Shell, husk or peel and trim. Some vegetables such as lima beans, corn-on-the-cob and asparagus require sorting for size since blanching times depend on the size of the pieces. Blanch vegetables to stop enzymatic action and reduce deterioration in color, flavor and texture. Most vegetables are blanched by heating them in boiling water for a specified time. A blancher, consisting of a tall stockpot, basket and cover, is convenient to use and can be purchased at most department or discount stores. However, any large pan, which can be fitted with a wire or perforated metal basket and cover may be used.

To ensure adequate water blanching, immerse a basket containing a small amount of the vegetable (about one pound) into large amount of boiling water (at least one gallon). Start timing once the water returns to a boil. Blanching time will vary with the vegetable and the size of the pieces, so follow the recommended blanching times for each vegetable.

Cool blanched vegetables by immersing them in a large quantity of cold water (60°F or below). Rapid cooling is necessary to stop the food from cooking. Cool the vegetable for about the same length of time as it was blanched. Once cooled, drain the cooled vegetable thoroughly before packaging. A large colander is useful for draining.

INDIVIDUALLY QUICK FREEZING (IQF) VEGETABLES

Spread blanched vegetables on a tray (i.e. cookie sheet) making sure pieces do not touch one another. Place tray in rapid freeze section or directly on the bottom (near coils) of the freezer. If pieces are small, vegetables will freeze in 1 to 2 hours. Mix frozen vegetables together as desired. Package vegetables and label. Store at 0°F or lower in home freezer.

Blanching Times for Vegetables (after water returns to a boil)

Vegetable	Preparation	Blanching Time
Asparagus	Wash, trim and discard tough parts; leave whole or cut	Small spears – 2 minutes Large spears – 4 minutes
Beans, Lima	Shell, wash and discard hulls	Small seeds – 2 minutes Large seeds – 4 minutes
Beans, Snap, String, Italian, green and wax	String beans, snap ends, cut to desired length; wash well	Small pods – 2 minutes Large pods – 3 minutes
Beets (without tops)	Wash, trim tops and root to ½-inch	Until tender – 25 to 30 minutes. Cool, slip off skin and cube or slice
Broccoli	Wash, trim from stalk; wash again cut into 1½-inch florets	3 minutes in salt water (4 teaspoons Mrs. Wages® Pickling & Canning Salt per gallon of water)
Brussels Sprouts	Trim off coarse leaves and stem	4 minutes in salt water (4 teaspoons Mrs. Wages® Pickling & Canning Salt per gallon of water)

Blanching Times for Vegetables (after water returns to a boil) (continued)

Vegetable	Preparation	Blanching Time
Cabbage	Discard loose outer leaves. Wash and quarter or cut into wedges	Quarters – 3 minutes Wedges – 1½ minutes
Carrots	Wash, remove tops, peel and slice or dice	Sliced or diced – 2 minutes Whole – 5 minutes
Cauliflower	Break into 1 to 2-inch pieces; wash	3 minutes in salt water (4 teaspoons Mrs. Wages® Pickling & Canning Salt per gallon of water)
Corn, Sweet (kernels)	Husk; remove silk, wash and trim off defective kernels. Blanch, cool then cut from cob.	4 minutes
Eggplant	Wash, peel and slice ⅓-inch thick	4 minutes in 1 gallon water + ½ cup lemon juice
Greens (spinach, beet, kale, mustard)	Wash 3-4 times or until water is clear; remove diseased/ discolored leaves	2 minutes
Peas (shell or green)	Shell, sort and wash	1½ minutes
Peas (sugar snap)	Snap ends and remove strings; wash	1½ minutes
Peppers (sweet, all types)	Wash, remove stem and seeds. Place whole/pieces on tray. Freeze overnight; package and return to freezer.	None needed
Pumpkin and Winter Squash (for purée)	Wash, slice, remove seeds and fiber	Steam, boil or bake until tender. Peel and discard skin; mash/purée flesh.
Squash, Summer Zucchini	Wash and slice as for serving	Until tender (3 minutes)
Squash, spaghetti	Wash, slice in half, scoop out spaghetti flesh and discard skin	3 minutes

NOTES

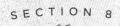

Home Canning

GUIDE AND RECIPES

BLUE RIBBON RECIPES

IOWA, ILLINOIS AND MINNESOTA STATE FAIR FAVORITES: BLUE RIBBON RECIPES

Here at Mrs. Wages®, we maintain the high standard for fine fruit and vegetable canning that began when Mrs. Wages first sold her pickling lime from her general store in Tupelo, Mississippi, in the mid-20th Century.

In honor of her legacy and to keep the canning flame alive among veteran and new canners alike, Mrs. Wages® sponsors the annual canning competitions at many of the largest state fairs including Iowa, Illinois and Minnesota State Fairs. Competitors earn their blue ribbons and we could not be prouder.

We believe all canners should be able to preserve the best of the harvest and share that blue-ribbon goodness with family and friends.

In this chapter, meet a few of the blue ribbon winners and the recipes that won judge's hearts from the Iowa, Illinois and Minnesota State Fair canning competitions.

These winners share a love for food preservation, a high standard for quality ingredients, and a belief that the art of canning should be preserved for future generations.

ILLINOIS STATE FAIR
BEST OF SHOW – JELLY

BEST OF SHOW BASIL JELLY
By Shawn Sechrest, Bloomington, IL

"I thought I'd go out on a limb and do something weird!
I've entered plain jellies, but harvested some sweet basil
from my garden and lo and behold, it wins!

"My uncle taught me to can, but he recently passed away.
He would have been so proud to win. This was my first year without
him and my first blue ribbon for jelly. It has a sweet and savory taste.
Drizzle the jelly on a brick of cream cheese and enjoy!"

- 4 cups water

- 2 cups firmly packed fresh basil leaves, finely chopped

- 1 package powdered fruit pectin

- 3 drops green food coloring (optional)

- 5 cups sugar

Combine water and basil in a large saucepan. Bring to boil. Remove from heat. Cover and let stand for 10 minutes. Strain and discard basil. Return 3⅔ cups liquid to pan. Stir in pectin and food coloring. Return to a rolling boil over high heat. Stir in sugar. Boil for 1 minute, stirring constantly. Remove from heat. Skim off foam. Carefully ladle hot mixture into hot half-pint jars, leaving ¼-inch headspace. Wipe rims and adjust lids. Process for 15 minutes in a boiling water canner.

Yield 6 half-pints

ILLINOIS STATE FAIR – SAUCES

BLUE RIBBON "RAISE THE ROOF" BBQ SAUCE
By Dianna Wara, Washington, IL

"My whole project one summer was to learn how to can, but I've been tinkering with barbeque sauces for a long time. I couldn't believe I won with my first try! The winning sauce entry is an original recipe. The onions and the chili peppers come from my own garden. At home we like to use habaneros, but I toned it down for the judges."

- 1 cup strong brewed coffee
- 2 cups ketchup
- 1 cup cider vinegar
- 1 cup firmly packed light brown sugar
- 2 cups finely chopped onions
- 4 cloves garlic, peeled and crushed
- 5 fresh jalapeño peppers, seeded and finely chopped
- 4 tablespoons dry mustard mixed with 2 tablespoons water
- ¼ cup Worcestershire sauce
- 4 tablespoons ground cumin
- 1½ tablespoons Mexican chili powder

1. Combine coffee, ketchup, vinegar, brown sugar, onions, garlic, peppers, mustard mix, Worcestershire sauce, cumin, and chili powder in large stockpot. Mix well. Bring to simmer over medium-high heat. Reduce heat and simmer for 20 minutes. Remove from heat. Purée mixture in a blender or food processor until smooth. Ladle hot sauce into hot pint jars. Adjust seals and caps. Process for 20 minutes in a boiling water canner.

Yield: 2 pints

ILLINOIS STATE FAIR – BEST PRESERVES

BEST OF SHOW BLUE RIBBON MANGO PRESERVE
By Linda Cifuentes, Mahomet, IL

"I found a peach preserve recipe and just substituted the mango.
I just knew it'd place. The golden orange color is beautiful and
the fruit is so well distributed throughout and not clumpy.

"This preserve is delicious. Put it on toast or cook with it.
I use it as glaze for chicken and pork chops.
It's nice with jalapeño and cilantro, too.

"Every year I can with my 76-year old bachelor
uncle up at his Wisconsin lake house. He will pick up canning jars on sale
all year long, and when I stay, I can there and give him some to keep."

- **4 cups peeled and chopped mango**

- **juice of one lemon**

- **6 cups granulated sugar**

- **1 pouch Mrs. Wages® Liquid Fruit Pectin**

---

1. Wash half-pint jars in hot soapy water. Sterilize in boiling water for 10 minutes and hold in hot water.

2. Place mangoes, lemon juice, and sugar in large pan. Bring to boil. Add Mrs. Wages® Liquid Fruit Pectin and return to boil for 1 minute. Remove from heat and let rest for 5 minutes to prevent fruit from floating. Ladle into sterilized jars and process in water bath for 5 minutes.

Yield: 8 half pints

ILLINOIS STATE FAIR – CANNED FRUITS – PEARS

BLUE RIBBON PEARS IN TURBINADO SUGAR SYRUP
By Ken Pitman, Waverly, IL

"The secret to this winning recipe is using raw sugar. It has a bigger crystal and carries a lot of molasses with it. I use the same amount as any granulated sugar. It's just got a unique taste and gives the pears a real pretty beige color. As for pear varieties, this year I used 'Golden Pear' although 'Bartlett' works, too.

"We have our own fruit orchard that I planted about 15 years ago. I'm retired now, but still love to can after watching my mother can the same her whole life."

- 2¼ cups Turbinado (raw) sugar
- 5¼ cups water
- 9 pounds pears (medium size works better for tight pack)

1. Cook sugar and water over medium heat, stirring until the sugar melts. Bring to boil.

2. Wash, peel and core pears, cut in half or quarters. Place in Mrs. Wages® Fresh Fruit Preserver to prevent discoloration. Use a strawberry huller to remove the seeds and veins. A melon baller will work but does not have a serrated edge, and a strawberry huller does.

3. Hot Pack: In a large saucepan, add drained pears to boiling medium syrup. Bring mixture back to boil. Boil pears for 5 minutes. Remove from heat and place hot fruit and syrup in hot 1-pint jars leaving ½-inch headspace. Remove air bubbles with a non-metallic tool. Wipe jar rim clean. Place hot lid on the jar and screw band down evenly and firmly. Process jars for 20 minutes in a boiling water bath. Remove from canner and let jars cool in a draft free area until sealed.

Yield: about 8 pints

ILLINOIS STATE FAIR – CANNED FRUITS – CHERRIES

BLUE RIBBON CHERRIES
By Ken Pitman, Waverly, IL

"My secret is to use black cherries. I use a medium syrup because they are a sweet cherry. I hot pack them and just follow the USDA guidelines. They look so good when you put them in a jar.

"We have our own fruit orchard that I planted about 15 years ago. I'm retired now, but still love to can after watching my mother can the same her whole life."

- **6 pounds dark sweet cherries (dark cherries make a very appetizing product)**
- **2¼ cups sugar**
- **5¼ cups water**

---

1. Wash, remove stems and pit cherries, leaving whole. May place pitted fruit in Mrs. Wages® Fresh Fruit Preserver to minimize browning at the pitting site. With dark cherries, this is not a problem. Cook sugar and water over medium heat stirring until the sugar melts. Bring to boil.

2. Hot Pack: In a large saucepan, add cherries to boiling medium syrup. Bring mixture back to boil, heating cherries thoroughly. Remove from heat and place hot fruit and syrup in hot 1-pint jars leaving ½-inch headspace. Remove air bubbles with a non-metallic tool. Wipe jar rim clean. Place hot lid on the jar and screw band down evenly and firmly. Process jars for 15 minutes in a boiling water bath. Remove from the canner and let jars cool in a draft-free area until sealed.

Yield: about 6 pints

ILLINOIS STATE FAIR – CANNED FRUITS – PEACHES

BLUE RIBBON PEACHES IN HEAVY SYRUP

By Ken Pitman, Waverly, IL

"I have tried spiced peaches, but by the time you hot pack them, they are overripe. One year I bought California peaches. You want to minimize bruising and handling and use them when they are firm but not soft. By the time you've peeled, pitted and cooked them, they can get too soft and the edges will be "feathery." (The judges told me that trick.)

We have our own fruit orchard that I planted about 15 years ago. I am retired now, but still love to can after watching my mother can the same her whole life."

- 10 pounds peaches: any variety will do as long as they are ripe but firm to touch; "Freestone" is easier to use.
- 3¼ cups sugar
- 5 cups water

1. Wash, peel and remove the pits from the peaches, may leave in halves or slice. To prevent darkening, keep peeled fruit in Mrs. Wages® Fresh Fruit Preserver. I prefer to peel the peaches with a peeler. However the peaches may be peeled by dipping the fruit in boiling water for 30 to 60 seconds until skins loosen. Dip quickly in cold water and slip off skins. (I think this method tends to soften the fruit and makes it slippery and hard to handle.) Cook sugar and water over medium heat stirring until the sugar melts. Bring to boil.

2. Hot Pack: In a large saucepan, add peaches to boiling medium syrup. Bring mixture back to boil. Remove from heat and place hot fruit and syrup in hot 1-pint jars leaving ½-inch headspace. Remove air bubbles with a non-metallic tool. Wipe jar rim clean. Place hot lid on the jar and screw band down evenly and firmly. Process jars for 20 minutes in a boiling water bath. Remove from the canner and let jars cool in a draft free area until sealed.

Yield: about 6 pints

ILLINOIS STATE FAIR – BEST OF SHOW RELISHES

BEST OF SHOW ZUCCHINI RELISH
Submitted by Pam McGowan, Rochester, IL

Pam McGowan won Best of Show for her relish recipe at the 2013 Illinois State Fair and shares her secrets with us…

"I grow most of my own ingredients for this recipe. I use the relish on hot dogs, brats, burgers, and even in egg and tuna salad. Really, it's good just to eat it right out of the jar! I've also used my zucchini with Mrs. Wages salsa and it's delicious!"

- 10 cups coarsely chopped zucchini (unpeeled)
- 4 cups chopped onion
- 4 tablespoons salt
- 2½ cups vinegar
- 2 tablespoons celery seed
- 1 tablespoon black pepper
- 1 tablespoon nutmeg
- 1 tablespoon turmeric
- 2 tablespoons cornstarch
- 6 cups sugar
- 2 cups chopped celery
- 3 cups chopped bell peppers (red, yellow, orange, green)

1. In a large mixing bowl, stir chopped zucchini, chopped onion and salt together. Let the mixture stand overnight. Transfer to a colander to drain. Rinse under cold water. Squeeze out the excess water and place mixture in large stock pot.

2. Stir in the vinegar, celery seed, black pepper, nutmeg, turmeric, cornstarch and sugar. Bring the mixture to a very low boil, reduce heat and cook gently for 30 minutes. Add the chopped celery and chopped bell peppers. Cook for an additional 30 minutes.

3. Spoon the relish mixture into pint jars, seal and process in boiling water bath for 15 minutes.

Yield: 8 to 10 pints

ILLINOIS STATE FAIR BEST OF SHOW – JAMS, JELLIES AND PRESERVES

BEST OF SHOW APRICOT-PINEAPPLE JAM
Submitted by Brazilla Leonard, Harvel, IL

"We've been entering the Illinois State Fair for generations. We love it. I went to a local farmer's market and they had fresh apricots. I was trying to think of something unique. The lemon juice brings the flavor and color out of the apricots. I've been canning for 32 years. We are a farm family so we try to grow our own fruits and vegetables or buy local. This would be a great recipe to fill your Christmas cookies with."

- 5½ cups prepared fruit
  (About 2½ pounds of apricots and 1½ pounds of pineapple)

- ½ cup fresh lemon juice

- 8 cups granulated sugar

- ½ teaspoon butter

- 1 package Mrs. Wages® Fruit Pectin Home Jell®

1. Pit unpeeled apricots. Finely chop or grind apricots. Measure exactly 3 cups of prepared apricots into an 8-quart saucepan.

2. Cut, peel and core pineapple, and finely chop. Measure exactly 2½ cups of prepared pineapple into saucepan with apricots. Mix well.

3. Add lemon juice. Add pectin and butter and stir over high heat until it reaches a full boil.

4. Add sugar and stir thoroughly until it reaches a full rolling boil. Continue cooking for 4 minutes, stirring constantly to avoid scalding.

5. Ladle immediately into sterilized jars, filling to within ¼-inch headspace. Wipe jar rims and threads.

6. Cover with two-piece lids. Screw bands tightly. Place jars in hot water bath and process for 10 minutes.

Yield: 8 half-pints

ILLINOIS STATE FAIR – CANNED VEGETABLES

BLUE RIBBON WHOLE PICKLED BEETS

By Duane Renko, Edwardsville, IL

"This is an old family recipe, handed down from my wife's grandmother.
It is older than old! The key ingredients are the spices and dash of horseradish.

"I get the small young beets straight out of the garden. Friends and
family ask me for more year after year. I have been canning most of my life
and watched my grandparents do the same down on their farm."

- **6-7 pounds small young beets**
- **2 cups granulated sugar**
- **1 teaspoon ground allspice**
- **2 cups water**
- **2 cups strong vinegar**
- **1 teaspoon cinnamon**
- **Horseradish**

1. Wash beets and trim stems to 1-inch. Cook beets until tender, dip into cold water. Remove skins and stems.

2. To make syrup, combine sugar, allspice, water, vinegar, and cinnamon. Stir well to dissolve sugar. Pour syrup over beets. Bring to boil. Reduce heat and simmer for 15 minutes. Pack beets into hot jars leaving ½-inch headspace. Add dash of horseradish to each jar for variety. Cover beets with hot syrup leaving ½-inch headspace. Wipe rims and adjust lids. Process for 30 minutes on rack in boiling water bath. Set jars on wire rack or towels to cool.

Yield: 7 pints

IOWA STATE FAIR – MRS. WAGES® CANNING COMPETITION

BLUE RIBBON MRS. WAGES® KOSHER DILL PICKLES
By Rod Zeitler, Iowa City, IA

"I have been pickling for about 10 years. Mrs. Wages makes it a lot easier than the old way. I grow my own pickling cucumbers and look for the perfect length of about 4-inches."

- 10 pounds pickling cucumbers (4-inches long)
- 1 pouch Mrs. Wages® Kosher Dill Pickles Mix
- 3¹/₃ cups white vinegar (5% acidity)
- 7¹/₃ cups water
- 4 garlic cloves, peeled and sliced

1. Wash cucumbers and trim blossom ends. Drain. Leave whole, cut into spears or slice. In a large stainless steel pot, combine Kosher Dill Mix, vinegar, and water. Bring mixture just to boil over medium heat, stirring occasionally, until mixture dissolves.

2. Pack cucumbers into hot, sterilized pint jars leaving ½-inch headspace. Add 1 garlic slice per jar. Ladle pickling solution into each jar maintaining ½-inch headspace. Remove air bubbles. Wipe the rims with a clean damp cloth. Place hot lids and rings. Pickles were processed in a boiling water bath for 5 minutes.

3. Pickles were processed in Johnson County, IA, altitude 660 ft. Pickles canned in compliance with current USDA guidelines.

Yield: 7 pint jars

IOWA STATE FAIR – MRS. WAGES® CANNING COMPETITION

RED RIBBON SPICY DILL PICKLES

By Sandy Kinzenbaw, Marengo, IA, second place

"I like my pickles a bit spicy, so I have added the red pepper flakes.
The judge said she could definitely taste them. I've been using Mrs. Wages for
the past five or six years, and I love the pickle and salsa mixes. I'm a beginner at
pickling, but enjoy it. I get my cucumbers from local farmer's markets."

- **9-11 pounds pickling cucumbers (3 to 4-inches long)**
- **1 pouch Mrs. Wages® Kosher Dill Pickle Mix**
- **3⅓ cups white distilled vinegar (5% acidity)**
- **7⅓ cups water**
- **Red pepper flakes**

Note:
These will be fairly spicy. May use ⅛ teaspoon pepper flakes to make them a little less spicy.

1. Wash cucumbers and remove the blossoms and ends. Combine Kosher Dill Pickle Mix® with vinegar and water as directed on Kosher Dill Pickle package. Bring mixture just to boil over medium heat (use an aluminum pot). Stir constantly until mixture is dissolved.

2. Pack sliced or quartered cucumbers into sterilized jars. Add ¼ teaspoon of hot pepper flakes into the jars. Pour hot pickling mix into jars leaving ½-inch headspace. Remove air bubbles. Cap jars with sterilized jars and lids. (Note: If more liquid is needed for proper headspace, add a mix of 1 part vinegar to 2 parts water.)

3. Process for 5 minutes for pints and 10 minutes for quart jars in a boiling water bath canner. Remove and cover jars with a towel to keep cool air from hitting hot jars. Test and make sure all jars have sealed. If a jar has not sealed place in refrigerator and eat within 2 weeks. Pickles will be ready to eat after 24 hours.

Yield: 7 quarts

IOWA STATE FAIR –
PICKLED VEGETABLES WINNER

WHITE RIBBON PICKLED VEGETABLES
Submitted by Susan Schultz, Haverhill, IA

"I use Mrs. Wages for pickling. This entry featured California blend of vegetables, red pepper, pearl onions and celery. Also, this recipe is a great do-ahead before a family dinner without canning. Put it on your relish tray."

- 1 large bag California Blend vegetables (in your freezer section)
- 12 pearl onions
- 1 red, orange or green sweet pepper cut into chunks
- 1 stalk celery cut into chunks
- 1 pouch Mrs. Wages® Quick Process Kosher Dill Pickle Mix
- 3⅓ cups vinegar (5% acidity) (I divide the vinegar to ½ cider vinegar to ½ white vinegar)
- 7⅓ cups water
- Hot red pepper flakes
- Garlic cloves
- Peppercorns

1. Wash and sterilize pint jars.

2. Remove vegetables from the freezer and place in a bowl while jars are sterilizing.

3. Chunk peppers and celery and add to vegetables along with pearl onions. Toss vegetables to mix.

4. Heat Mrs. Wages® Kosher Dill Pickle mix, water and vinegar to a boil over medium heat.

5. To each jar, add ⅛ teaspoon each red pepper flakes and whole black peppercorns and one clove of garlic.

6. Fill jars with vegetables and ladle hot liquid over them, leaving ½-inch headspace. Seal with hot sterilized lids.

7. Place in a hot water bath and process for 5 minutes.

Yield: 6 pints

MINNESOTA STATE FAIR – JAM WINNER

WHITE RIBBON STRAWBERRY RHUBARB JAM

Submitted by Christine Robertson, Champlin, MN

"A friend of mine wanted to learn how to make this jam so we both made our batches. She is now hooked and wants to learn more about home canning. I enjoy this in yogurt. My husband has it on toast. I am going to try using it in thumbprint cookies."

- 4 cups crushed strawberries
- 2 cups chopped rhubarb
- ¼ cup fresh squeezed lemon juice
- 1 package of Mrs. Wages® Fruit Pectin Home Jell®
- 5½ cups sugar
- ½ tablespoon butter

1. Combine strawberries, rhubarb, lemon juice and Mrs. Wages® Fruit Pectin in a large saucepan.

2. Bring to a boil over high heat. Add sugar, stirring until dissolved.

3. Return to a rolling boil and add butter. Boil hard for 1 minute, stirring constantly.

4. Remove from heat, skim foam if necessary.

5. Ladle hot jam into prepared jars, leaving ¼-inch headspace. Adjust two-piece caps.

6. Process 10 minutes in a boiling water canner.

Yield: 6 half-pints

MINNESOTA STATE FAIR – JAM WINNER

RED RIBBON GOOSEBERRY JAM
Submitted by Marc Eaton, St. Paul, MN

"I love to make jams and jellies and sell at our neighborhood farmer's market
in St. Paul. I go and pick the berries at local farms as they come into season.
I enjoy this flavor. It's a simple recipe and I like mixing it with a plain yogurt.
It's also great on toast, bagels, and I've heard some folks like to put it on ice cream."
It was the first time I entered the fair and it's so exciting!"

- **8 cups gooseberries, tipped and tailed**
  (this results in 4 cups prepared gooseberry pulp)

- **6 cups granulated sugar**

- **1 pouch 3 fluid ounces Mrs. Wages® Liquid Fruit Pectin**

- **½ teaspoon vegetable shortening**
  (optional – this is a non-dairy method to reduce foaming)

Preparing the gooseberries:

1. Place 4 cups of the gooseberries into a food-mill and process to de-seed and de-skin.

2. Repeat with the second 4 cups of the gooseberries.

3. Measure out 4 cups of the resulting gooseberry pulp and set aside.

Making the jam:

1. Prepare boiling water canner. Sterilize clean jars. Keep sterilized jars and lids in simmering water until needed.

2. Place gooseberry pulp, shortening and sugar into a large saucepan.

3. Stir the mixture constantly and bring it to a rolling boil.

4. Add the Mrs. Wages® Liquid Fruit Pectin.

5. Return the mixture to a rolling boil, stirring constantly.

6. Boil for 1 minute, continuing to stir.

7. Remove from heat.

continued on next page

8. Ladle the mixture into hot jars, skimming foam, if needed, and leave a ¼-inch headspace.

9. Clean the jar rims and place lids/bands

10. Process as directed based on your altitude (10 minutes)

11. Remove jars and cool

12. Check seal on lids 24 hours later, Enjoy on toast, in yogurt or on ice cream

Yield: 8 half-pints

NOTES

NOTES

NOTES

NOTES

NOTES

NOTES

NOTES

THE ONLY COMPLETE LINE OF
FOOD PRODUCTS FOR PRESERVING FOODS

HOW TO ORDER MRS. WAGES PRODUCTS

Ordering Online www.mrswages.com

Visit our website www.mrswages.com for a complete product listing and description. Orders can be placed via the web site using your Discover, Visa or MasterCard credit card. It's fast, easy and convenient.

Call toll-free 800-647-8170

Phone in your order, have your Discover, Visa or MasterCard information handy.

Ordering Gifts?

The Mrs. Wages Home Canning Guide makes a great gift. We'll ship your Gift Orders to another address; simply give us shipping instructions when you order.

11457 Olde Cabin Rd., St. Louis, MO 63141
www.mrswages.com • 800-647-8170